Teacher's Copy

SOME EQUIVALENT MEASURES

	Metric	EXACT	APPROX.
WEIGHT	15 g	0·52 oz	½ oz
	25 g	0·88 oz	1 oz
	50 g	1·76 oz	2 oz
	100 g	3·53 oz	4 oz
	200 g	7·06 oz	8 oz
	300 g	10·59 oz	12 oz
	½ kg (500 g)	17·64 oz	1 lb
	1 kg	35·27 oz	2-2¼ lb
LIQUID MEASURE	140 ml	0·25 pint	¼ pint
	280 ml	0·49 pint	½ pint
	420 ml	0·74 pint	¾ pint
	560 ml	0·98 pint	1 pint
	1 litre	1·76 pints	1¾ pint
LENGTH	6-8 mm	0·24-0·31 in.	¼ in.
	12-14 mm	0·47-0·55 in.	½ in.
	25 mm (2½ cm)	0·98 in.	1 in.
TEMPERATURE	See table on page 33 for equivalence of degrees Celsius and Fahrenheit and Gas Marks.		

g=gramme kg=kilogramme ml=millilitre mm=millimetre cm=centimetre

Adventures in Cookery 1

MARGUERITE PATTEN

INTRODUCTION

I have planned this book so that by the time you have finished it you will be able to produce quite a number of meals that I hope you, and other people too, will enjoy. We eat every day; and one important thing about good food is that it is there to be enjoyed, through its *taste*, its *colour*, its *smell*. Another important thing about food is that it helps to keep us well. On pages 7-9 you will find why certain foods are good for you as well as pleasant to eat.

Be prepared to try new foods. Some flavours you will enjoy more than others, but it is interesting to eat foods that have a variety of flavours, and it is far more fun to cook many different dishes than to stick to just a few. After all, life would be very dull if we always wore the same coloured dress and always did our hair in exactly the same way. Meal times too are much more interesting if you have changes.

In your cookery lessons, you will learn to choose foods sensibly so that you do not waste time and money; then you will practise serving the food in such a way that it looks interesting and it makes people *want* to eat it. If you enjoy cooking, your own home, when you have one, will be a much more pleasant and comfortable place.

All measurements are given in this book by the metric system which you will be using in school as this is the ***Modern*** way of weighing and measuring. This has meant careful testing of the recipes again to make sure that all details are correct.

You will use this book in conjunction with your cookery lessons. Your teacher will tell you how she wants the various foods prepared, and the order in which you work, but I hope you will also enjoy it enough to want to try cooking at home. When you have made one dish successfully a first and second time, you may be able at home to add your own touches, to make it a little more interesting or exciting.

MARGUERITE PATTEN

Fifth impression 1972 107206
(Second metric impression)
ISBN 0 602 22008 4
Published in Great Britain
by Ginn and Company Ltd
18 Bedford Row, London WC1R 4EJ

(Title page) Roast potatoes (page 90)
(Left) Beef and vegetable casserole (page 167)

ACKNOWLEDGEMENT is made to the owners of coloured photographs used in this book as follows: Baco Foil Advisory Bureau (p. 91), Alfred Bird & Sons Ltd. (p. 20), British Egg Information Service (p. 37), Cadbury Bros. Ltd. (p. 146), Cheese Bureau (p. 56), Coffee Publicity Association (p. 38), Delrosa (p. 74), Flour Advisory Bureau Ltd. (pp. 73, 164), Fruit Publicity Council (pp. 109, 110, 145, 181), H. J. Heinz & Co. Ltd. (pp. 163, 199), Herring Industry Board (p. 127), Jobling Housecraft Service (p. 2), Kraft Foods Ltd. (p. 200), New Zealand Lamb Information Bureau (p. 92), Potato Marketing Board (pp. 1, 55), South African Co-operative Citrus Exchange Ltd. (p. 182), White Fish Authority (pp. 19, 128).

Thanks are due to the following for the use of black and white photographs: AEI-Hotpoint Ltd. (p. 21), Australian Home Cookery Service (p. 99), Alfred Bird & Sons Ltd. (pp. 103, 107, 195, 197), Baco Foil Advisory Bureau (p. 18), Blue Band Margarine (p. 173), Birds Eye Foods Ltd. (p. 68), British Egg Information Service (pp. 44, 45, 57, 58), Brown & Polson Ltd. (p. 79 both), Cadbury Bros. Ltd. (pp. 75, 76, 77 left, 81), Californian Prunes (pp. 60, 104, 202 left), The Cheese Bureau (pp. 48, 66 top, 72, 86, 149, 150, 153, 155), Coffee Publicity Association (pp. 50, 203), J. & J. Colman Ltd. (pp. 89, 166), Delrosa (p. 77 right), Flour Advisory Bureau (pp. 78, 84, 138, 147, 174, 175, 176, 177, 178, 189, 190, 191 all, 192, 196), Fruit Publicity Council (pp. 111, 131 bottom, 132, 161, 184 both), H. J. Heinz & Co. Ltd. (pp. 59, 66 bottom, 137, 157), Herring Industry Board (pp. 124, 126, 129 top, 194 both), The Honey Bureau (p. 62), Jobling Housecraft Service (pp. 17, 26, 167), Laconite (p. 35), Monogram Blanket Co. Ltd. (p. 30), National Milk Publicity Council (p. 69), New Zealand Lamb Information Bureau (p. 93), Pig Industry Development Authority (p. 96), Potato Marketing Board (pp. 13, 102, 159, 160, 168), Prestige (p. 15), Quaker Oats Ltd. (p. 61), Radiation Ltd. (pp. 27, 28 both), Rowntrees (pp. 130, 131 top), Simplex Electric Co. Ltd. (pp. 29, 30, 36), Spanish Fruit Syndicate (pp. 133, 134, 202 right), Stork Cookery Service (pp. 136, 140, 141, 142, 143, 144 both, 186 both, 187, 193), Surprise Peas (Batchelors) (p. 67), Sutton & Sons Ltd. (pp. 63 all, 64 all), Tupperware Ltd. (p. 16), T. Wall & Sons (Meat & Handy Foods) Ltd. (pp. 52, 54, 101, 183), White Fish Authority (pp. 117, 119, 121, 129 bottom), Women's Advisory Council on Solid Fuel (pp. 31, 32).

The author and publishers also gratefully acknowledge the expert advice given at all stages in the preparation of this course by Miss Winifred Hargreaves, formerly H. M. Staff Inspector, Home Economics.

Printed Offset Litho in Great Britain by Cox & Wyman Ltd, London, Fakenham and Reading

CONTENTS

Body building foods
Fats
OIL
BUTTER
Calcium
Carbohydrates
FLOUR
HONEY
Iron
Vitamins

CHAPTER ONE

Choosing foods

AS well as making appetising meals, the food we eat plays a big part in keeping us well. As you grow older, you will want a clear skin, good teeth, shining hair, and a figure that is neither too fat nor too thin. We cannot completely control these by food, for other things too affect our bodies; but if you eat food that is good for you, as well as interesting, you are helping to build and keep a healthy body.

Eating for health is not difficult

It means eating a variety of foods every day, choosing something from each of the following groups.

Body-building foods

You find them in

eggs, cheese, meat, fish, milk,
peas, beans, lentils

Generally called *proteins*, their purpose is to help children grow strong and well, and to keep grown-up people strong. They do *not* make you fat.

Fats

You find them in

butter, margarine, cooking fat, oil; fats in meats; herrings and other oily fish such as sardines, salmon

These foods create warmth. Without them our bodies feel the cold.

Carbohydrates—or sugars and starches

You find starches in

flour and anything made with flour, e.g. cakes, biscuits, macaroni; some vegetables, e.g. potatoes

You find sugars in

sugar itself, honey, golden syrup

These foods help create energy. Although we need a certain amount, it is a mistake to eat too much of them, for they spoil your appetite for more important foods. If you eat starches and sugar too often or in too great a quantity, *they make you fat and harm your teeth and skin.*

Iron

You find it in

liver, heart, kidney; bread, flour; eggs; cocoa; black treacle; dried fruits such as apricots, prunes; dark green vegetables like spinach, watercress

This mineral is essential for healthy red blood. A lack of iron gives anaemia, which makes you look very pale, and feel tired and unwell. You must also eat foods that contain vitamin C (described below) because this vitamin helps the body to use the iron in foods containing it.

Calcium

You find it in

milk, cheese

This important mineral helps in building bones, allowing teeth to grow, and keeping the whole body strong and healthy.

Vitamin A

You find it in

fatty fish such as herrings, butter, margarine, eggs, liver, carrots, green vegetables

This is necessary for growth. It also helps to give a clear healthy skin and good eyesight. If you need extra amounts of vitamin A, you take cod liver oil, or halibut liver oil.

Vitamin D

You find it in

the same foods as under vitamin A except those that do not contain fat

It is often found together with vitamin A. It is very important for good formation of bones and teeth. Sunlight also provides the body with vitamin D.

Vitamin B

You find it in

wheat germ, yeast (both in bread), yeast extract such as marmite

It helps to prevent a feeling of overtiredness.

Vitamin C

You find it in

green vegetables, *properly cooked (overcooking destroys this vitamin)*; potatoes —especially when new; fruit—in particular oranges and other citrus fruits; black currants; rose hips; strawberries

This is most important. In the old days, when sailors on ships lacked vitamin C, they developed a very bad skin disease called scurvy. Vitamin C foods help to give you a clear skin and to build up resistance to illness.

You will notice that some foods are found in several groups. Eggs, for instance, come under body-building foods, iron and vitamin A. Bread and flour come under carbohydrates, iron and vitamin B. As your teacher will explain to you, only sugar itself belongs to just one group.

When, at the end of each section in this book, you are asked what is the main food value, that is the main *nutrient*, in the foods you have used, you will need to refer to the groups described here.

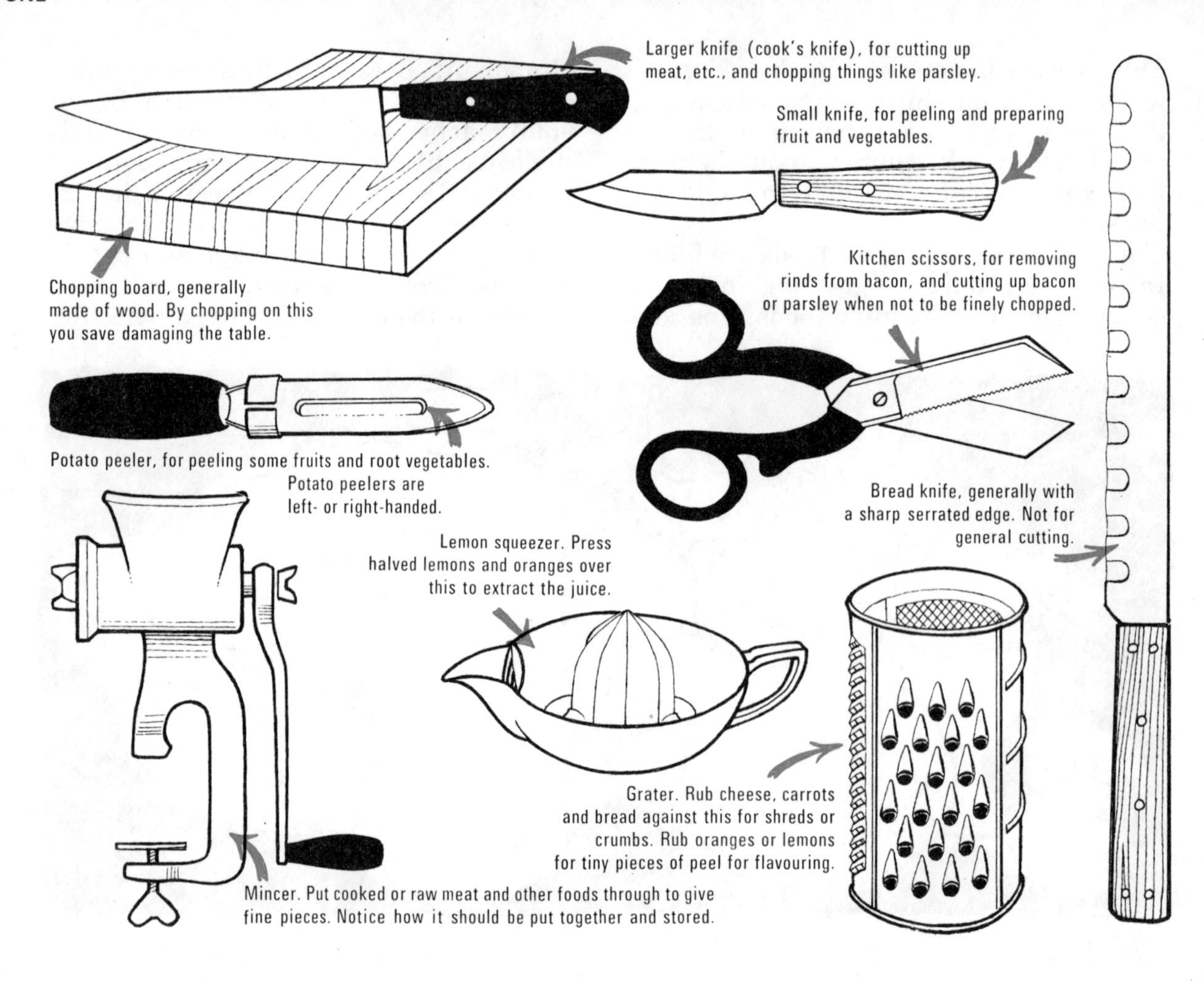
Larger knife (cook's knife), for cutting up meat, etc., and chopping things like parsley.
Small knife, for peeling and preparing fruit and vegetables.
Chopping board, generally made of wood. By chopping on this you save damaging the table.
Kitchen scissors, for removing rinds from bacon, and cutting up bacon or parsley when not to be finely chopped.
Potato peeler, for peeling some fruits and root vegetables. Potato peelers are left- or right-handed.
Bread knife, generally with a sharp serrated edge. Not for general cutting.
Lemon squeezer. Press halved lemons and oranges over this to extract the juice.
Grater. Rub cheese, carrots and bread against this for shreds or crumbs. Rub oranges or lemons for tiny pieces of peel for flavouring.
Mincer. Put cooked or raw meat and other foods through to give fine pieces. Notice how it should be put together and stored.

CHAPTER TWO

Use and care of kitchen tools and utensils

THESE are some of the tools and utensils that will probably be in your housecraft room at school, or your kitchen at home. Most of them are expensive to buy, so they should be looked after carefully.

They need to be thoroughly washed after use. Add the right amount of washing-up powder or liquid to hot water in a bowl or in the sink.

You will be told in your first lessons the order in which you should wash things up. Remember this as it will save time.

Tools for cutting, etc.

To clean

First remove stains from knives, etc. with steel wool or abrasive cleaner. (Stainless knives should not need this.) Scrub chopping boards to remove stains. Brush away tiny pieces of food from sides of grater, cutters of mincer, top of lemon squeezer.

Wash in hot washing-up water and dry carefully, taking care that the sharp edges do not cut your fingers. Put in a warm place for a while before storing. Plastic lemon squeezers should be washed in warm water only.

If knives become blunt

they cannot do their work properly. You will be shown how to sharpen them.

When you buy knives

1. Choose a knife you can hold easily. If it is too large or too heavy you cannot control it well.
2. Choose a good quality knife. Cheap ones become blunt easily and have to be replaced quickly.
3. Decide whether you want knives that can be sharpened. For knives that 'work hard', such as a cook's knife, it is a good idea to have the type that can be sharpened. The serrated edge type will become blunt after hard use, and you cannot sharpen this yourself.

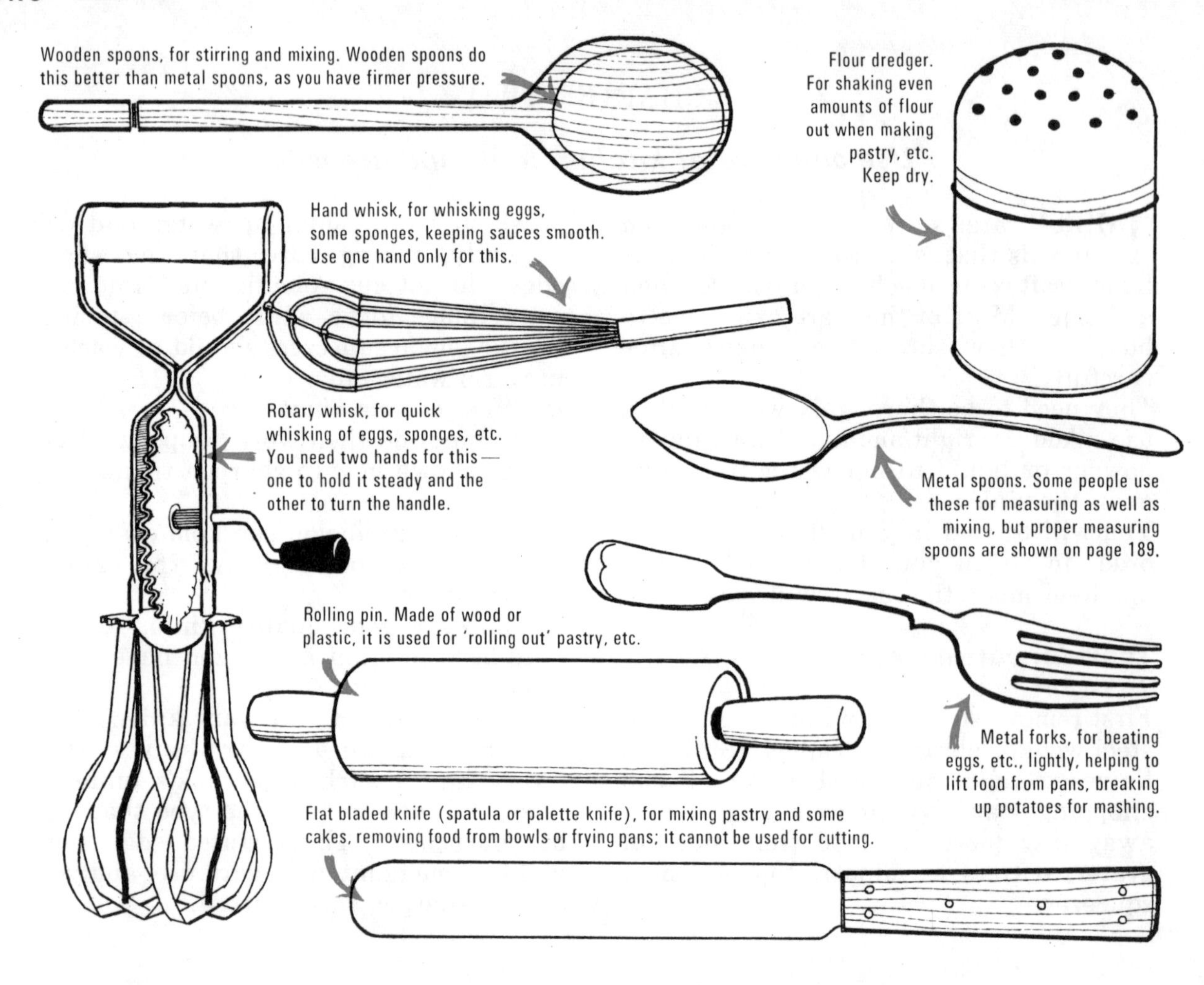
Wooden spoons, for stirring and mixing. Wooden spoons do this better than metal spoons, as you have firmer pressure.
Flour dredger. For shaking even amounts of flour out when making pastry, etc. Keep dry.
Hand whisk, for whisking eggs, some sponges, keeping sauces smooth. Use one hand only for this.
Rotary whisk, for quick whisking of eggs, sponges, etc. You need two hands for this— one to hold it steady and the other to turn the handle.
Metal spoons. Some people use these for measuring as well as mixing, but proper measuring spoons are shown on page 189.
Rolling pin. Made of wood or plastic, it is used for 'rolling out' pastry, etc.
Metal forks, for beating eggs, etc., lightly, helping to lift food from pans, breaking up potatoes for mashing.
Flat bladed knife (spatula or palette knife), for mixing pastry and some cakes, removing food from bowls or frying pans; it cannot be used for cutting.

Using a potato peeler. Normally the peel would be gathered in a piece of newspaper and thrown away, or put into a pig bin

Tools for mixing and handling foods, etc.

To clean

Remove stains first, then wash in hot water; if plastic, use warm water. If fish slice is enamel, take care it does not chip. Wooden spoons and rolling pins must be put in a warm place before storing. The rotary whisk *must not* be put completely into water; keep the top part containing oil dry.

Fish slice, for turning and lifting food from the frying pan.

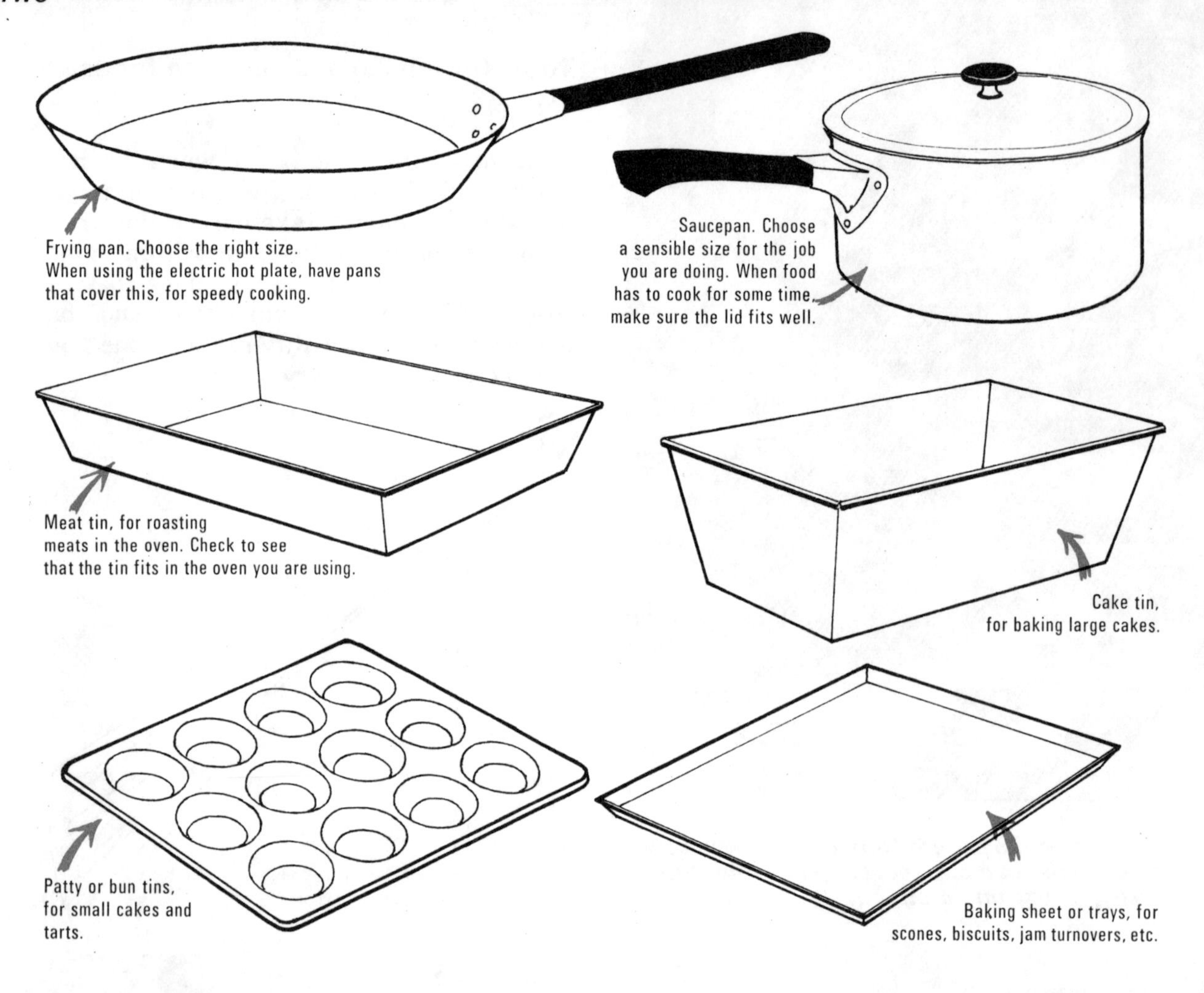
Frying pan. Choose the right size.
When using the electric hot plate, have pans that cover this, for speedy cooking.
Saucepan. Choose a sensible size for the job you are doing. When food has to cook for some time, make sure the lid fits well.
Meat tin, for roasting meats in the oven. Check to see that the tin fits in the oven you are using.
Cake tin, for baking large cakes.
Patty or bun tins, for small cakes and tarts.
Baking sheet or trays, for scones, biscuits, jam turnovers, etc.

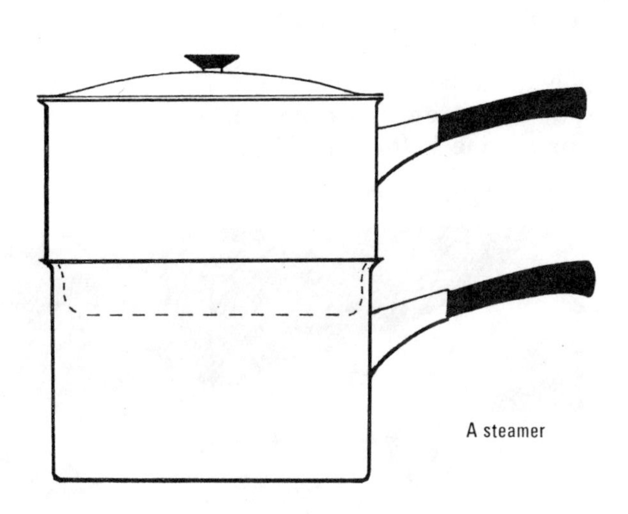
A steamer

To clean
Put pans to soak after use. Always use cold water for pans that have cooked egg or milk dishes. Wipe out greasy pans with kitchen paper before soaking and washing. Wash pans and tins in warm or hot water using a pan scourer or nylon pan brush. Dry well and put all tins in a warm place to dry off thoroughly before storing. Your teacher will tell you if there are some cake tins she prefers not to wash.

Utensils for cooking, etc.
In addition to the utensils opposite, you will probably have a steamer, so that puddings can be cooked in this over a pan of boiling water. You will also have pan stands to protect the table, and wire cooling trays on which to put cakes, scones and biscuits when they come out of the oven.

One way of hanging saucepans

Colander, for draining liquid from vegetables. The holes are too large for sieving.

Sieve, used to take the lumps out of food. Push the food through firmly into a bowl. Also used for sieving flour, etc.

Strainer. Small strainers are used for tea and coffee. Larger ones are for straining gravy.

Tools for straining, etc.

To clean

Clean as saucepans, etc. Be careful to put sieves and strainers in a warm place for a time before storing.

Special combined salad shaker and colander

Other things found in your housecraft room

Ovenproof glassware (see above)

Many pie-dishes, plates and casseroles are made in this ware. If food has stuck round the edge, put the dish to soak before washing it in hot water. Never bring a casserole out of a hot oven and put it on a wet or cold surface.

China and glassware

In addition to ovenproof glassware, you will have china mixing bowls and basins. You will also use china plates and dishes, glassware for drinking, glass bowls and glasses for serving food. Take care not to overheat china or pottery dishes when warming them. Wash them in plenty of warm water. Glasses need careful washing and drying, then polishing to give a clear look. Your teacher will tell you how to do this.

Tables

You will either work on wooden tables or tables with laminated plastic surfaces. Wooden-topped tables should be washed then well dried. If badly marked, clean with a scrubbing brush and soapy water. If you put hot pans on to wooden tables you will mark them. Always use a pan stand or asbestos mat. Laminated plastic-

(Above) Stuffed cutlets of cod (page 193)
(Opposite) Grilled cod cutlets and halved tomatoes, lemon wedge and parsley (page 119)

topped tables, or as they are sometimes called, Formica-topped tables, are made so that you can stand warm things on them, but do not put very hot frying pans, saucepans or meat tins direct from the oven on the table. They will mark or even melt the surface. Use a pan stand or asbestos mat. *Never* place a hot iron on the table. You can *cut* on this type of table, but do *not chop*. Use a board. You will probably use a pastry board for rolling out pastry, etc.

Foil
Aluminium foil, sold in rolls, is used for covering food, in cooking and storing. It helps to keep food moist both in cooking and in the refrigerator. After use, it can be washed and dried ready for using again.

Sinks
Take a pride in keeping the sink clean. Use washing-up liquid and abrasive cleaner where necessary. If the sink is of white enamel, do not bang pans in it as they mark and chip the sink. A little household bleach and abrasive cleaner will remove most marks. Stainless steel

sinks need careful washing and drying. A porcelain sink can be kept a good colour with abrasive cleaner.

Draining board and taps
Clean in the same way as the sink, scrubbing the wooden boards well. Rub the chromium taps with a dry duster to give them a good shine.

Cooker (See page 34.)

Refrigerator
This is generally cleaned when defrosting. (See page 206.) Always return foods to the clean refrigerator in the shortest possible time.

Dish cloths and tea cloths
Wash these out well in the hottest detergent solution your hands will bear. It is better to use a washing machine and first wash, then boil, tea cloths. If stained with fruit juice or other liquids, your teacher will tell you how to remove or loosen stains. Do not put a tea cloth in hot water when badly stained without first soaking or loosening the stain.

(Above) Refrigerator after being defrosted

(Opposite) Jellies (page 130), Instant Whip pudding (page 83), Dream Topping (page 82)

CHAPTER THREE

Weighing and measuring ingredients

YOU may hear some people say that they *never weigh* or they *never measure*. This is not the easiest or best way to cook, because you get results that are different each time. If you make a cake today, and it turns out exactly right, you will want the same result next time. You can only get this by weighing the ingredients carefully, handling them in the right way, and baking at the right temperature. (*Ingredients* are the different foods that go to make up a recipe.)

Weighing

In your housecraft room you will have *scales*. If they are the type *with weights*, remember these points:

1. Make sure that the scale pan is quite clean. The scales may have been used for weighing cheese and somebody may not have wiped the pan properly.
2. Make sure the scales are standing quite flat. If they are tipped on a sloping draining board, you do not get the correct balance and cannot weigh accurately.
3. Choose the weight you want; put it on the scale. Add the food to the scale pan fairly slowly. If you put it in too quickly, you may pour on too much and waste time in putting it back into the container.
4. When the pan drops to the level of the side holding the weights (picture 2), you have exactly the right weight. If it is higher (picture 3), you have too little food;

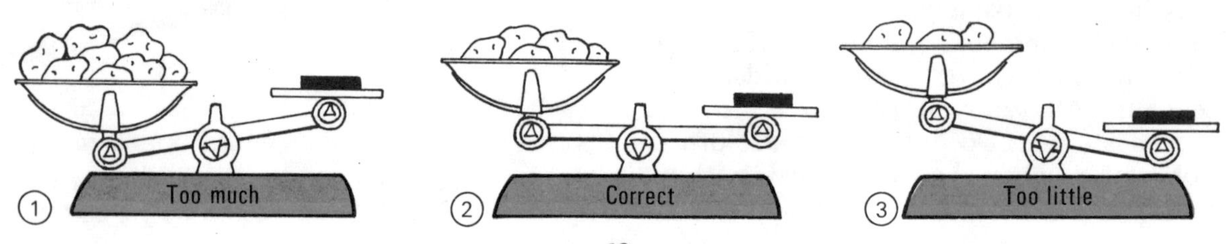

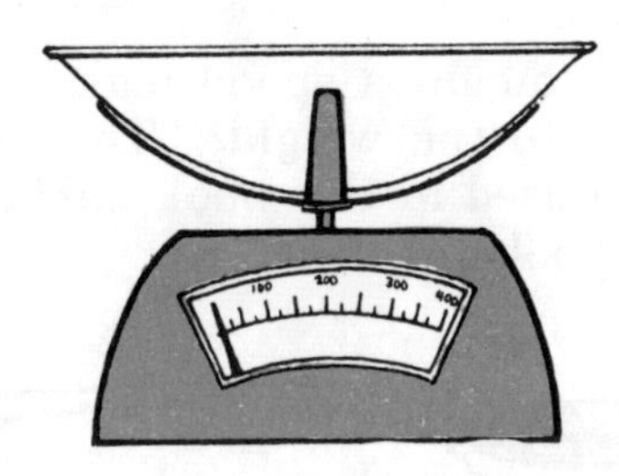

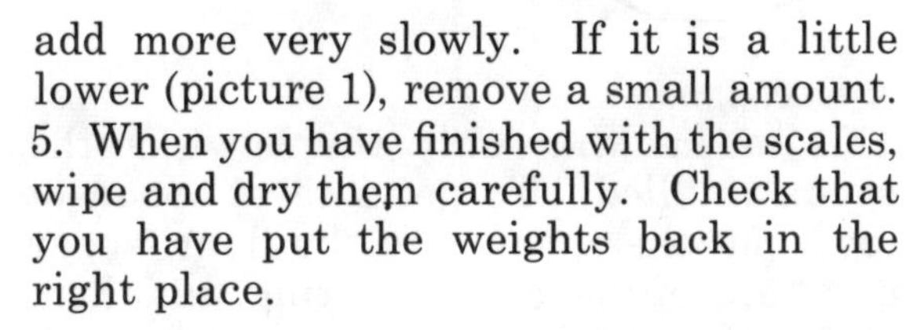

add more very slowly. If it is a little lower (picture 1), remove a small amount.
5. When you have finished with the scales, wipe and dry them carefully. Check that you have put the weights back in the right place.

Scales of the *balance type* have no weights. You weigh by putting food into the scale pan until the indicator points to the weight you need.
1. Make sure the balance scales stand on a completely flat surface.
2. Check that the indicator or pointer is at zero (0). When you carry these scales the indicator sometimes moves. You may have to ask how to set these particular scales. It is generally done by turning a small knob which makes the indicator return to zero.

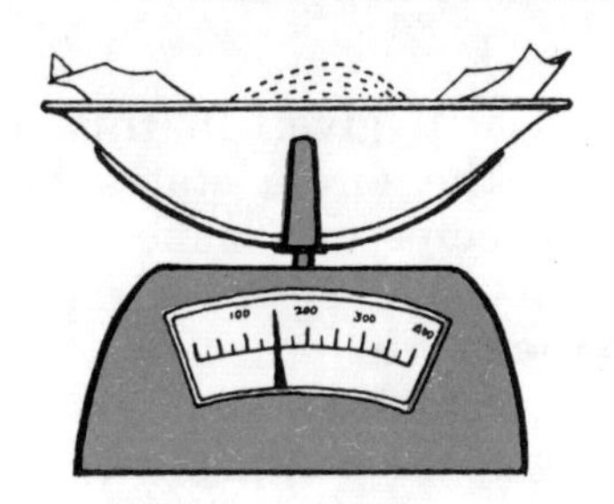

3. Put the food into the scale pan.
4. Stand directly in front of the scales so that you can see where the pointer is. If you stand to one side, you will not read it correctly.
5. If you need 100 grammes the pointer should be on the 100.
6. When you have finished with the scales, wipe and dry them carefully.
7. If you put balance scales into a cupboard, make quite certain that nothing heavy is against them to cause damage.

When weighing foods, it is a good idea to place a piece of greaseproof paper on the scale pan, and put the butter, cheese, or whatever food is being weighed, on to this. Lift the paper and the food off together.

When you plan a recipe, always make certain that you know the number of portions it will give. In this book, the number in the circle states how many helpings a recipe will make.

How to measure

Although weighing food is the most accurate way of making sure you have the right amount, sometimes it is easier to measure. If all the class wanted the scales at the same time, it would mean a long wait, or you may be in a kitchen where there are no scales. Try to use scales for really essential things like weighing the ingredients for making pastry or a cake.

Measuring with a spoon

The spoon to use for measuring is a tablespoon. There are measuring spoons designed by the British Standards Institute (B.S.I.) which ensure accurate measurement. Many people use ordinary tablespoons. If you compare several of these you will find that they vary in size. As some are bigger than others, you are likely to get measurements that are not quite correct. Use the B.S.I. measuring spoon whenever you can.

The way you fill a spoon makes a lot of difference to the weight. The following terms are used in this book, and in other cookery books as well.

A level spoon

This means that only the bowl of the spoon is filled. To get a level spoon of food, put the spoon into the flour, sugar or whatever you are measuring, and then, with a flat knife, scrape any extra back into the container.

A rounded spoon

If a recipe mentions a rounded spoon, it means that you should have as much food above the bowl of the spoon as you have below. This is *not* the best way of measuring, however, as it is easy to make a mistake and have too little or too much.

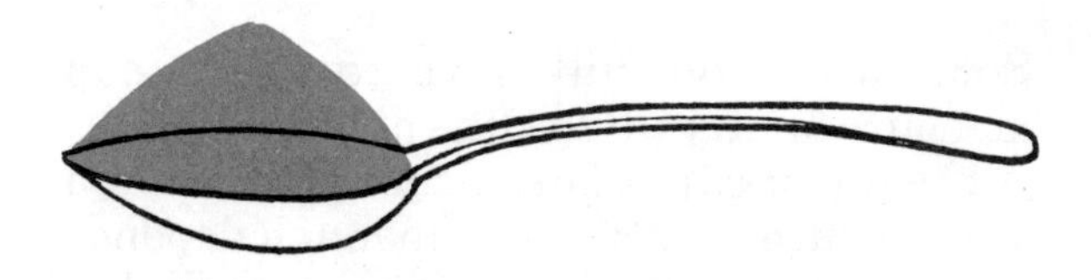

A heaped spoon
This means that you have as much in the spoon as it will hold. It is not a good way to measure because when the spoon is so full it is difficult to handle.

Teaspoon measures are obtained in the same way.

25 g flour = 3 *absolutely* flat tablespoons
If you do not level them with a flat knife, it is safer to use just 2 tablespoons.
25 g cornflour as flour
25 g cocoa as flour
25 g sugar (castor or granulated) = $1\frac{1}{4}$ level tablespoons

Measure the level tablespoon first. Put it on to a plate or in a basin. Fill the spoon again and level it off. Then, with your knife, mark the sugar into quarters. Tip the quarter spoon in with the level tablespoon.

25 g icing sugar = 2 level tablespoons
25 g jam or golden syrup = $1\frac{3}{4}$ dessertspoons
15 g gelatine = 1 level tablespoon
25 g cheese = 2 level tablespoons finely grated cheese
15 g fat = 1 level tablespoon

A pinch
Many recipes mention 'a pinch' of salt. This means picking up as much salt as you can between your forefinger and thumb.

A shake
Sometimes a recipe will talk about 'a shake' of pepper. This means just shaking the pepperpot *once* over the ingredients in a saucepan or a basin.

Take care when you weigh or measure ingredients. If you use more or less of certain ingredients than the recipe says *you could have a failure.*

How to measure with a cup

When a recipe says 'a cup of milk', in this country we mean a breakfast cup which holds about 280 ml.

Some B.S.I. measuring jugs are available but you may not have one in your kitchen and will have to rely on breakfast or tea cups. If you look at different kinds of teacups you will find they vary in size a great deal. This is why a teacup is not a good measure.

Sometimes you will have to use a cup measure for dry things like flour and sugar. A breakfast cup is best although it is not a very accurate measure. So much depends on the way you pack it. It is best to fill the cup loosely and not press it down.

1 breakfast cup of flour holds approximately 100 g.

1 breakfast cup of sugar holds approximately 200 g.

1 breakfast cup of dried fruit holds approximately 200 g.

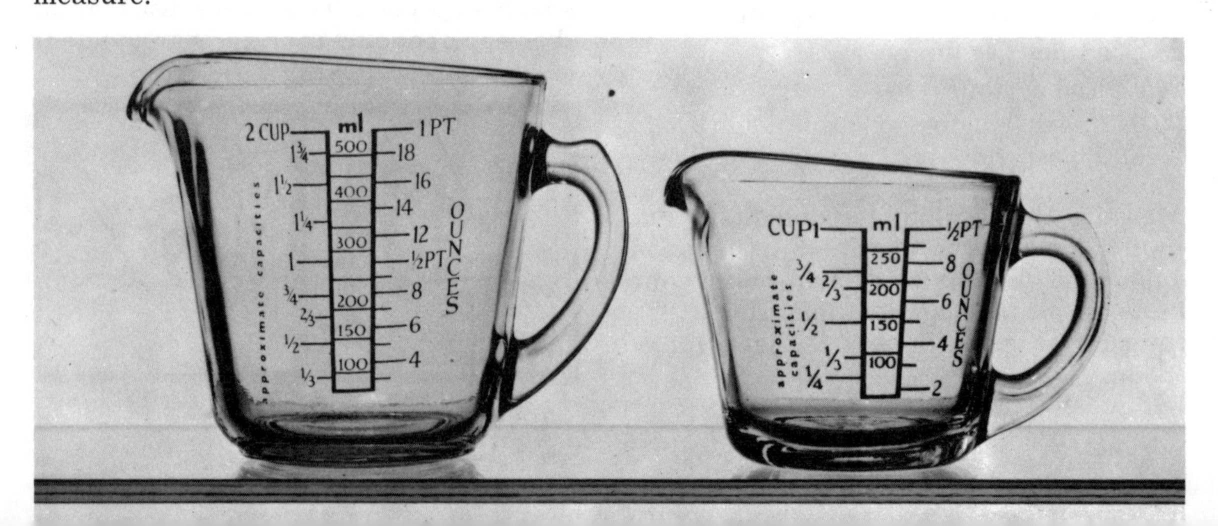

CHAPTER FOUR

Temperature control and timing

THE cooker is the most important piece of equipment in the kitchen. It is worth while, therefore, taking time to understand how to control it properly. Whichever cooker you use, read the manufacturer's chart carefully. The temperatures given in this chart are average only. They do vary and you must learn the differences in each individual cooker.

Using the gas cooker

To get the right temperature in the oven
First light the oven and then set the indicator to the right number. Wait 15–20 minutes for the oven to reach the required temperature. Unless your teacher or the recipe tells you to alter the oven setting during cooking, there is no need to touch it again; the oven remains at this temperature.

Placing food in a gas oven
The top of the gas oven is the hottest part; the bottom is the coolest part. This means that if you have three dishes to cook, the food which needs the greatest heat goes at the top, the dish requiring the next hottest part of the oven is put in the centre, and the dish requiring the least heat goes at the bottom.

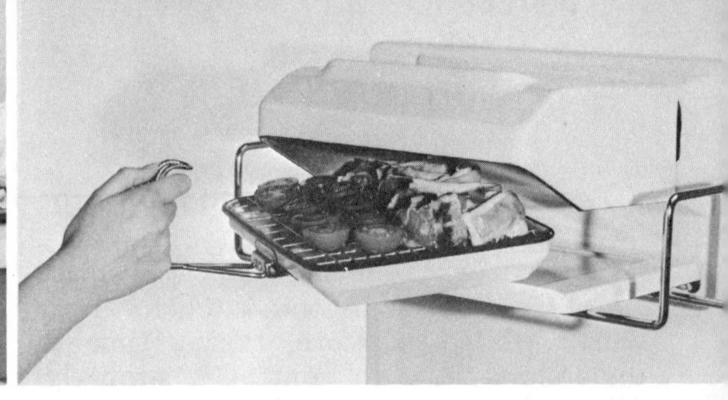

Using the gas rings
Light the gas. You may have a cooker with automatic ignition, or a lighter attached, or you may have to use a taper. Remember to turn the gas down when you start cooking. If a recipe says *simmer* only (see page 43), you will have the gas very low. Never have the gas flame coming up the sides of the saucepan. On some modern gas cookers there is a device which can be set to give you exactly the right amount of heat for frying, boiling or simmering.

Using the gas grill
Light the grill. When cooking most foods, it is best to allow the grill to heat for several minutes before placing the food underneath. The one exception is bacon. To stop it curling badly, put the bacon under the grill before lighting it. When food begins to brown, if it is not completely cooked, you may have to turn the gas down or move the grill pan away from the heat.

Using the electric cooker

To get the right temperature in the oven
First switch on the electricity both at the main control panel and at the cooker. Set the oven, or thermostat switch, to the temperature required. The oven has reached this temperature when the light goes out. It will take approximately 15–20 minutes, according to the temperature required. The oven stays at this temperature throughout cooking.

Placing food in an electric oven
Although electric ovens vary slightly, most of them are hottest at the top, nearly as hot at the bottom, and coolest in the centre. This means that if you have three dishes to cook, the food needing the greatest heat is put at the top, the dish requiring the next hottest part of the oven at the bottom, and that requiring the least heat in the centre.

Using the electric boiling plates
Switch on the boiling plate. Generally, one uses the highest number or setting to bring food to the boil and then turns it down to a lower number or setting. Notice carefully the number you need for simmering, or boiling steadily on a cooker, and when you use this again, you can set to the same number. Some electric cookers have a device which can be set to give you exactly the right amount of heat for frying, boiling or simmering.

Using the electric grill
Switch on the grill and leave for a few minutes to become really hot. The only exception is for grilling bacon. (See *gas grill.*) When the food begins to brown, you may have to turn the grill down to low or a lower setting, or even move the grill pan further away from the heat.

Using an automatic timing device
Many modern electric cookers and a few gas cookers are fitted with an electric timing device. This enables you to set the oven to switch on at a certain time, and cook the food. It switches itself off at the end of the cooking time. Your teacher will explain more fully how to

set this. It is quite simple, but it needs care the first time you use it.

Using an electric kettle
When heating water in an electric kettle, the elements must always be covered, even when boiling the water for small quantities of tea or coffee.

Using a solid fuel cooker

To get the right temperature in the oven
To do this, you must spend time learning how to fill, clean and adjust the cooker. Your teacher will help you, and it is important to read the maker's instruction book very carefully.

Placing food in a solid fuel oven

Most solid fuel cookers have two ovens: the cooking, or, as it is often called, the roasting oven, and the simmering or plate warming oven. The top oven is the hotter, and although you will follow the directions for placing food in the oven, it is a help to know that the hottest part of the oven is towards the top, with the bottom part of the oven next hottest, and the centre the coolest. (See picture below.) The simmering oven may be used for the very long slow cooking of casseroles and milk puddings. (See picture, page 32.)

A solid fuel cooker, showing the roasting and warming ovens

Using the solid fuel plates

You will generally have two types of plates on a solid fuel cooker. The boiling plate, which is for quick cooking, and the simmering plate for slower cooking. It is possible to bring foods to the boil quickly and then to transfer them to the simmering plate. To get good results on the top of a solid fuel cooker, really thick, heavy pans must be used. Close the lids over the boiling and simmering plates after use.

Grilling with a solid fuel cooker

For grilling meat on a solid fuel cooker, you can generally obtain special pans. The grilling is done by putting the pan over the heat instead of having heat coming from above, as with gas or an electric cooker. (See picture, page 32.) For toasting, the bread is put between two wire racks and put *over* the heat.

Careful timing in cooking

It is very important to time cooking carefully. Sometimes food takes a little longer or a little shorter time to cook than given in the recipe because the cooker may be slightly hotter or cooler than average. Get into the habit of looking at the food just before the end of the cooking time.

If you cook food more quickly than given in the recipe, you may burn it. Meat may become hard and dry.

If you cook food too slowly, cakes, for example, may not rise or brown; meat, fish and vegetables will not be cooked at the end of the time given.

If you cook food for too long a period it becomes dry and will not taste pleasant.

If you cook food for too short a period it will be under-cooked.

Controlling oven temperatures

When you use the cooker at home, you become used to the temperature of that particular oven, and know at what heat it should be set for every kind of dish.

In your housecraft room at school you will be using a number of cookers—gas, electric and solid fuel. You will find the ovens vary. In one gas cooker you may use Mark 3 for a certain dish, but in a different make of cooker you will need Mark 4. The same applies to electric cookers. This means that the numbers and temperatures given in this table and in the recipes are *the most usual* or average settings only. When baking cakes and pastry, you must be particularly careful about oven heat and should look at the chart *belonging to that particular cooker* before you put on the oven. Check that the number is *right* for the oven you are using.

In an electric oven, heat is given thus:
400°F. or (in future) 200°C.

° means degrees; F. means Fahrenheit; C means Celsius, which is the modern way of giving temperatures. The *precise* conversion of degrees F. to degrees C would be too complicated for an oven dial so they are 'rounded' off as below.

In a gas oven, heat is given in numbers.

	ELECTRIC		GAS
	°Celsius	°Fahrenheit	Number
Very cool or	110 or 120	225 or 250	0 or ½
Very slow	120 or 135	250 or 275	½ or 1
Cool or slow	135 or 150	275 or 300	1 or 2
Very moderate	160 or 180	325 or 350	3 or 4
Moderate	180 or 190	350 or 375	4 or 5
Moderately hot	190 or 200	375 or 400	5 or 6
Hot	220 or 230	425 or 450	7 or 8
Very hot	230 or 260	450 or 500	8 or 10

CHAPTER FIVE

Cleaning the cooker

YOU will be taught how to remove parts of the cooker for easy cleaning. Each cooker varies slightly in the parts that will pull out, but you will soon learn about them. If a cooker is to work well it must be kept clean. Always switch off electricity or turn off gas before cleaning the cooker.

Here are other things to remember:

1. Whenever food boils over on top of the cooker, wipe it up at once.
2. You may also have to give the cooker an extra clean after cooking.
3. If you do not wipe up food when it is spilt, it may smell unpleasant and cause burning on the outside of the saucepan.
4. If food boils over when you are cooking, you are using too great a heat. Watch this carefully and turn the heat down.

Cleaning the oven

1. An oven is simple to clean if it is wiped out after use, while still hot. You will find hot water and detergent will keep the inside of the door and oven bright. If you have a glass door, wipe with a dry cloth while still warm.
2. You will need to give the oven regular special cleaning, removing all the shelves and as much of the oven lining as possible. Wash all parts carefully. Any marks on a glass door should be gently rubbed away with a little abrasive cleaner and soft cloth. Then rinse the door in clean water and dry.
3. If foods spill over in the oven, the dish is too full or the heat too high.
4. If you are cooking foods with a lot of liquid such as a meat casserole or stewed fruit, it is wise to stand the cooking dish on a baking tray. If the liquid should boil over, it does not fall to the bottom of the oven.
5. If things are allowed to boil over in an oven they burn and create fumes and an unpleasant smell.

CHAPTER SIX

Care in the kitchen

THE food you will be handling, and in many cases cooking, will be eaten by other people as well as yourself. We all dislike food that is stale or has been prepared by people with dirty hands or cooked in a pan that is not quite clean.

Remember these points:

1. When you are shopping for food, buy it from a clean-looking shop.
2. When you bring it home, put it away carefully. Pages 205-212 give you correct storage for food.
3. When the time comes to use it, make certain that in all preparations and cooking you are very particular.

When you handle food have on a clean apron, overall or dress—something that can easily be washed if you happen to stain it.

Check that your hands are clean and well rinsed. If you have washed them with soap and not rinsed them afterwards you may give a soapy taste to food. Wash again after you have prepared meat, fish, vegetables or other foods. Always wash your hands after a visit to the toilet. Carelessness when handling food can cause food poisoning.

(Above) The warming drawer in a cooker
(Opposite) Egg salad (page 47), egg sandwiches (page 46), scrambled egg (page 57)

Is your hair brushed well back? At school you may be wearing a cap. At home, pin or tie it back when you cook, because when you are working your hair tends to fall forward. If you push it back with your hands, odd hairs might get on food, which is far from pleasant.

Check that the table top you are using is clean. If it is not, wipe it. Normally plates, saucepans, etc., *will* be clean, but look at them to make quite certain.

Some people who are very fussy about their kitchens and their food are far less fussy about dish cloths and tea cloths. This is very wrong. A dish cloth washes the utensils and china used when cooking and serving food, and it must be very clean. It is also unpleasant to use if it is greasy and dirty. Tea cloths should be washed frequently. They are then easy to clean. Your teacher will tell you how to do this.

Make a habit of being particular about buying food. Store, cover and handle food with care. When the time comes to use it, make certain your hands, clothes and utensils are clean.

CHAPTER SEVEN

The way you work

IT is difficult when you begin cooking to be as quick as you wish; that does not matter, for each time you make the recipe you will work more rapidly. From the first lesson try to work *tidily*. Your teacher will tell you the order in which to work; listen to her and follow her instructions.

First read the recipe. Then decide not only the food you need, but what sauce-pans, spoons, etc. Whatever your order of work, gather everything together for the recipe: (1) the food (2) equipment for making—spoons, basins, etc. (3) equipment for cooking—saucepans, etc.

This may *seem* to hinder you in starting to cook. Actually it will not. Once you have everything ready, you can work undisturbed. You will not have to stop during cooking. Just imagine if everybody had forgotten the same saucepan and all rushed to get one at the same time! When you cross the room to collect one article, save time and energy if you can by getting something else as well.

As you work, tidy up. Put food back in the cupboard. If you have used an egg, throw away the shell. Put vegetable peelings in the right place. As you dirty spoons and knives, wash them up. You may need them again in preparing a recipe. If you do not, put them neatly to one side on your table or put them back in the proper place.

Wipe the table *before* you start a second dish or dish up.

Do not work in a muddle. If you do, you will work more slowly and become more tired. The kitchen will look untidy, and this nobody likes.

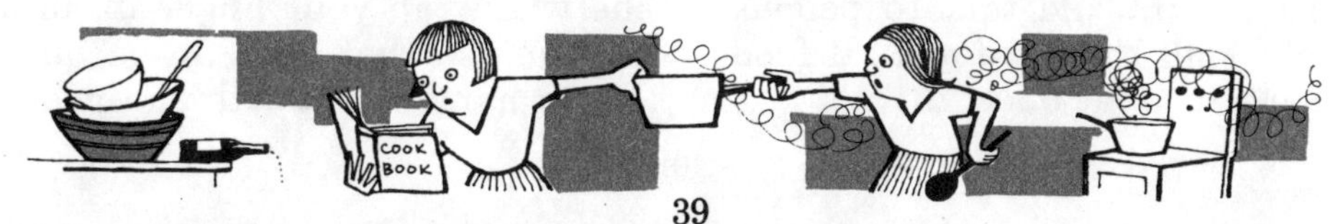

Left) Breakfast with coffee and boiled eggs (pages 45 and 50)

CHAPTER EIGHT

Safety in the kitchen

YOU have heard about the dangers in a home of fire and of people falling. Do you know that more accidents happen in the home than on the roads?

Most accidents can be prevented, so be careful when you work with pans of hot food where people are moving about.

1. Never light any burner on a gas cooker without seeing that all the other taps not in use are turned off. If one has been left on and you use a match or lighter, there might be an explosion. After using the cooker, turn everything off.

2. When you use an electric cooker, make certain that all hot plates not in use are switched off. If one has been left on, you could easily burn your hand, so turn off all switches after use.

3. When you carry filled pans, support them steadily and watch what you are doing. Do not turn and talk to people, for you might spill the hot food. If food is spilled, wipe it up at once.

4. When you leave pans on the cooker, check that all handles are turned towards the back of the cooker. Somebody passing could easily knock against the handle and tip the pan over.

5. Heat foods and liquids carefully, particularly when frying, as fat splashes when too hot. Listen when your teacher tells you the correct heat to use. If you spill fat on the cooker, wipe it up at once to prevent it from catching fire.

6. Before you bring hot containers of food to the table or sink, see that there is plenty of room for them to stand steadily. Use oven gloves to remove hot food from the oven. If you have burnt yourself, tell your teacher at once. Notice what she puts on the burn in case it happens again. If you cut yourself when working, let the teacher know. Probably she will wrap your finger in an adhesive dressing so that you can go on working. Never handle food with an uncovered cut.

CHAPTER NINE

Words used in cooking

IN every cookery book you will find certain words used over and over again. They form part of the ' language ' of cookery and it is important to understand them. You must know the number of portions a recipe will give. In this book it looks like this:

①= one portion; ④= four portions

Terms used in preparing dishes

Beating means mixing the ingredients together with a very brisk movement to incorporate air. Most people work clockwise, that is from right to left, and a wooden spoon is generally used.

Blending: mixing the ingredients together. The term used when flour, cornflour, etc. is mixed with a cold liquid, for example, in making cocoa or a white sauce by the blending method. (See page 69-70.)

Creaming: beating fat and sugar together until they are soft and fluffy.

Folding: adding an ingredient slowly and gently to others already beaten, to avoid losing air. Use a metal spoon or palette knife.

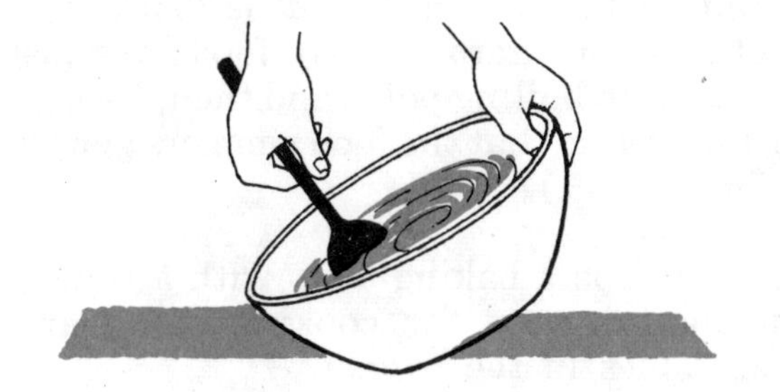

Kneading means working the ingredients lightly together with your hands by bringing the outside of the dough into the centre. This word is used in bread making; you will also find it mentioned in making biscuits. (Pages 139-140.)
Rolling out is a term used when making pastry, scones and some biscuits. Put the dough on to a pastry board or the table and roll lightly with a rolling pin until it becomes the required shape and thickness.

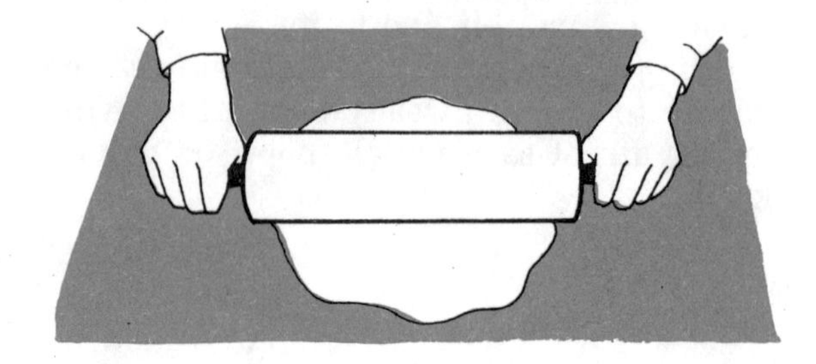

Rubbing in is a method of mixing fat with flour. Rub the fat into the flour with your fingers, until the mixture is like breadcrumbs. For recipes using this method see page 139.

Whisking: a very brisk, circular movement: to incorporate air, used for eggs and batters, generally with an egg whisk.

Terms used in cooking

Baking is cooking in the oven without fat. Cakes, pastry, biscuits and certain kinds of meat are baked.

Boiling is cooking in liquid at boiling point 100°. When liquid is boiling it bubbles very hard. Many foods are just brought to boiling point and then the heat is lowered so that the food simmers gently. (See page 43.)

Casserole is a baking dish, with a tightly fitting lid, used for cooking stews and vegetables in the oven.

Frying is cooking in fat. There are three kinds of frying; *dry frying,* cooking without additional fat, used for bacon and sausages; *shallow frying,* cooking in a little fat; and *deep frying,* cooking in a lot of oil or fat.

Grilling is cooking under the grill in a quick heat.

Roasting is cooking in the oven in fat. Some fat meat can be roasted in its own fat without extra fat being added.

Seasoning means adding salt and pepper.

Simmering is steady cooking in liquid. You should see an occasional bubble on the surface. The temperature for simmering is 82°–87° Celsius. Cover pans when simmering for a long time, otherwise the liquid evaporates.

Steaming is cooking over steam. The easiest way to do this is to stand the food in a steamer over a pan of boiling water. If you do not possess a steamer, put enough water into a saucepan to come half-way up a basin, and put on to steam. Take care to add more boiling water to the saucepan from time to time.

Stewing is cooking slowly by simmering in a little liquid, in a closed pan.

Warming—Hot foods should be served on hot plates or dishes. These can be warmed in racks on the top of the cooker or in a hot cupboard or warming drawer. If you ever warm plates in the oven, make certain the temperature is low.

These shortened forms are often used:

kg = kilogramme or kilogrammes
g = gramme or grammes

1. EGGS AS A MEAL

EGGS are one of the most important foods. They are a *protein food.* In Chapter One you read about proteins, and your teacher will explain more about them and how they help in building strong bodies and bones. Eggs are also one of the most *useful* of foods. They can be served as the main part of a meal or are used in making cakes, puddings and other dishes.

One of the simplest and nicest ways of cooking an egg is to boil it.

How to boil an egg

1 egg water	①

1. Take a rather small saucepan; you may have special egg saucepans.
2. Put in enough cold water to cover the egg (or eggs). This generally means that the saucepan is half filled.
3. Put the saucepan on the cooker to boil, but do not let the water boil away.
4. Take the egg in a basin (so that it does not fall) and a tablespoon over to the cooker.
5. Put the egg into the spoon, and lower it into the water carefully.
6. Immediately look at the clock, your watch, or the cooker timer (which your teacher or the cooker instruction card will tell you how to set).
7. Some people like to put eggs into cold water, bring to the boil and time from this

point. Because the egg *starts* to cook as the water comes to the boil, the cooking time is shorter.

	Really soft-boiled egg	Firm set egg	Hard-boiled egg
if put in cold water	3 minutes	4 minutes	10 minutes
if put in boiling water	4 minutes	5 minutes	10 minutes

8. Watch the time carefully. Remove the egg from the water, put into an egg-cup and serve immediately.

How to make an egg into a complete meal

Other things are needed besides an egg. At breakfast you have toast. With practice, you can make this while the egg is cooking, but at first it is better to make the toast and then to boil the egg.

How to make toast

1. Heat the grill for 1-2 minutes so that the toast browns quickly without becoming too hard.
2. Put a slice of bread on the grid of the grill pan.
3. Watch it as it browns on one side.
4. Turn it over and let it brown on the other side.
5. When the toast is ready, stand it up so that it does not become limp but stays crisp. This is best done in a toast rack.

You will also want to serve tea or coffee with the egg. (See pages 48-51.)

Eggs as a sandwich filling

①
1 egg
15 g butter or margarine
pinch salt, shake pepper
bread

1. Hard boil the egg for the time given in the table.
2. As soon as it is cooked, put it into a basin of cold water. At the same time, tap it to crack the shell. (This lets the steam out and prevents an ugly dark ring

forming round the yolk.) Allow the egg to get quite cold.
3. Remove the shell, put the egg into a basin and cut it into small pieces.
4. Add the butter or margarine, a pinch of salt and a shake of pepper.
5. Mash everything together with a fork. The mixture is then ready to spread on bread or bread and butter. (See picture, page 37.)
Other sandwich fillings are described on page 85.
An egg also turns a salad into a meal.

Hard-boiled egg salad

1 egg ①
2 or 3 lettuce leaves
1 tomato

1. Hard boil the egg and cool it.
2. While the egg is cooking, prepare the salad. Wash the lettuce leaves in cold water, shake them dry in a salad shaker over the sink or pat them gently between the folds of a dry clean tea towel. Arrange them on a plate or dish.
3. Put the tomato on a chopping board, cut into slices or quarters with a vegetable knife and arrange on the lettuce.
4. Cut the shelled egg into halves or quarters and put on top. Add mayonnaise if you wish.

Eggs are *one* body-building food. As you work through this book you will find a number of meals using other body-building foods. One of the most important is cheese. As a change from an egg salad, you can make a cheese salad.

Cheese salad

2 or 3 lettuce leaves ①
1 tomato
25–50 g cheese

1. Make the salad base in just the same way as for an egg salad.
2. You can put the *piece* of cheese on the salad, but it looks nicer if you grate it.
3. Stand the grater on a fairly large plate. Take the piece of cheese in your right hand, and rub it firmly up and down the coarse side of the grater.
4. Pile the grated cheese neatly in the centre of the salad. (See picture, p. 48.)

5. If you wish, you can use a hard-boiled egg as well as the cheese, and add mayonnaise.

Choosing cheese

On page 208 several types of cheese are mentioned. One of the best to use in a salad is Cheddar cheese.
Another quickly made salad is sardine.

Sardine or sardine and egg salad

A tin of sardines is more than enough for one person, so you will notice the salad ingredients have been increased to give enough for 2–3 people.

½ small lettuce
2 or 3 tomatoes
tin of sardines

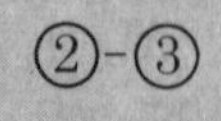

1. Prepare and make the salad.
2. Open the tin of sardines with the key. (If you have not already done this at home, your teacher will show you how.)
3. Lift the fish out of the tin with a small knife and arrange on the salad.
4. Add a hard-boiled egg if you wish. (See picture, page 37.)

How to make tea

The most important thing to remember is to take the teapot to the kettle, and not the kettle to the teapot. In this way you will be sure of pouring *really* boiling water on to the tea in the pot.

tea	milk
water	sugar

1. Pour water from the *cold tap* into the kettle and put it on to heat.
2. Take the teapot over to the kettle and when the water is hot, but not boiling, pour a little into the teapot to warm it.
3. Just before the water in the kettle is boiling, pour the water out of the teapot and put in the tea.
4. If you are making a pot for one person only, put in 2 level teaspoons.
5. We generally say ' one teaspoon per person and one for the pot '. If you are making a pot of tea for four people, you would put in 5 level teaspoons of tea for a really strong brew. If you like weak tea you can use a little less.
6. The moment the water in the kettle boils, turn or switch off the heat.
7. With an electric kettle, pull out the plug *after switching off the electricity.*
8. Hold the kettle firmly; then pour the boiling water steadily over the tea.
9. Put the lid on the teapot and let it stand for several minutes. Some people like to stir the tea, *then* let it stand.
10. The leaves fall to the bottom of the pot and the tea is ready to be poured, through a tea strainer if possible.

How to make coffee

There are a number of ways in which to make coffee. You may have a percolator or other coffee maker at home, but making it in a jug is a good way as well as an easy one.

ground coffee	milk
water	sugar

1. Put water, drawn from the cold water tap, on to boil.
2. For 1 cup of coffee we generally allow 140 ml so you can work out how much water to heat according to the number of cups of coffee you are preparing.
3. Allow about $\frac{1}{2}$ teacup of milk for each person.
4. To 560 ml of water you will often be told to use 2 rounded tablespoons of ground coffee. If you are practising using level tablespoons, see page 24; you will need to use 4.
5. Warm the jug for coffee as you warmed the teapot for tea.
6. Put in the coffee.
7. Pour on the boiling water.
8. Let it stand for 1 minute; then stir with a spoon.
9. Put a lid on the coffee jug. If you have no lid, use a folded tea cloth. Let the coffee stand for 5 minutes in a warm place.
10. While the coffee is standing, heat the milk but do not let it boil, for this spoils the flavour of coffee and the milk forms a skin, which most people dislike.
11. Some people prefer cold milk in coffee.

12. When the coffee is ready, pour it, through a strainer if you have one, into cups, or into a warm coffee pot.
13. If you have no strainer, pour *very carefully*, for although the coffee grounds sink to the bottom, some of them may rise if you pour too rapidly.
14. Add hot milk to each cup, or pour it into a separate jug and serve immediately.
Often people use what is called 'instant coffee' instead of ground coffee. To prepare this, you use about 1 teaspoon of instant coffee to each cup of water. You will find full instructions on the tin.

What foods will this meal give you?
Look at pages 7 to 9 and see just how good a meal you have prepared.

What nutrients are in these foods?

eggs cheese sardines
lettuce tomatoes
bread or toast and butter
tea or tea with milk and sugar
coffee or coffee with milk and sugar

2. BREAKFAST OR SUPPER

THE foods you are now going to cook can be served either for breakfast or supper. They include bacon, eggs, sausages and tomatoes.

Choosing bacon

In the 'shopping list' on page 207 you will find several kinds of bacon mentioned. You will probably be frying streaky or back rashers.

Fried bacon and egg

1 or 2 rashers bacon	①
1 egg	15 g (1 level tablespoon) fat

1. Put a plate or dish to warm.
2. Cut the rinds off the bacon with a sharp knife or kitchen scissors. This makes bacon fat crisp better. If the rashers are very long, cut into halves to fit into the frying pan.
3. Put the bacon rinds into the frying pan *with the bacon*, as they give extra fat for cooking the egg.
4. Light the gas or switch on the electric hot-plate, and cook the bacon until the fat is golden in colour. This usually takes about 3 minutes, but varies with the thickness of rasher. Thick rashers need turning over during cooking.
5. Lift the bacon on to the warmed dish with a fork or tongs, and remove the rinds. Keep the bacon hot.
6. Crack the eggshell sharply with a knife or against the edge of a saucer or cup.
7. Pull the halves of the shell apart so that the egg gently drops into the cup.

8. Put fat into the frying pan and heat until melted.
9. Pour the egg into the hot fat. If you are cooking several eggs in the same pan, put in one egg and turn the heat down when the white starts to set. Put in the second egg, and so on.
10. Cook the egg 2 minutes for a lightly set egg or 3 minutes for a firmer egg.
11. Bring the plate with the bacon near the frying pan.
12. Lift the egg out of the pan with a fish slice and arrange next to the bacon. Serve as soon as possible.
Many foods can be served with bacon.

Bacon and fried bread

1–2 rashers bacon ①
small slice bread

1. Cook the bacon and bacon rinds as before to stage 4.
2. Lift the bacon on to a hot dish.
3. Put the slice of bread into the frying pan and cook for 1 minute. Then turn and cook for another minute until crisp and brown.

Bacon and tomato

1–2 rashers bacon	salt	①
1 tomato	pepper	

1. Cut the rinds off the bacon and cut the tomato into halves.
2. Sprinkle the cut sides of tomato with a pinch of salt and a shake of pepper.
3. Put the bacon and bacon rinds into a pan. Cook 2 minutes for thin rashers; thicker ones will take longer.
4. When the bacon is nearly cooked, put in the tomato halves and cook for 1 minute. *Do not over-cook,* otherwise tomatoes lose flavour and texture.
5. Serve with the bacon.

Choosing sausages
(See shopping list, page 207.) You can buy both pork and beef sausages. Chipolata, a smaller variety, cook more quickly.

Bacon and sausages

1–2 rashers bacon ①
1 or 2 sausages

1. Put a dish to warm.
2. As sausages take longer to cook than bacon, these are cooked first.
3. Prick each sausage with a fork to stop the skins splitting.
4. Put into the frying pan without fat.
5. Cook slowly, turning the sausages round as they brown. Large sausages will take 15 minutes; chipolata sausages will take 10 minutes.
6. When the sausages are cooked, put on to the hot dish.
7. Cook the bacon and serve with the sausages. (See picture, page 52.)
8. Many people prefer to grill bacon and sausages. (See pages 98-100.)
9. Most people like mustard with sausages.

Breakfast and supper menus

For breakfast you will serve bacon and eggs or sausages or tomatoes and fried bread, with toast, butter, tea or coffee. Look back to pages 46, 48-51, to see how to make these.
What else would you have for breakfast? Why not start the meal with fresh orange juice, grapefruit, or cornflakes?
For supper you can serve bacon and eggs or sausages or tomatoes and fried bread, with bread and butter, tea or coffee. What else could you have with the bacon or tomatoes for supper?
Why not have a salad, or heat a can of baked beans or spaghetti. (See pages 47-48, 156-157 and picture, page 157.)

What nutrients are in these foods?

bacon bread eggs
sausages tomatoes

Mashed potatoes (page 101

3. MORE WAYS OF COOKING EGGS

THERE are other ways of cooking eggs apart from boiling and frying. (Pages 45-46 and 52-53.) Two of the most popular are scrambled and poached eggs.

How to scramble an egg

	①
1 slice bread	
little butter for toast	pinch salt
15 g margarine or butter	shake pepper
1 egg	1 dessertspoon milk
to garnish: small piece washed parsley	

1. Warm a plate.
2. Toast and butter the bread. Keep warm on the plate while cooking the egg.
3. Break the egg into a basin, add salt, pepper and milk, and beat with a fork.
4. Melt the margarine in a saucepan.
5. Add the egg and milk. Turn heat very low and cook slowly.
6. Stir with a wooden spoon, moving the egg from the bottom of the pan all the time, until the mixture begins to thicken.
7. Remove pan from heat, for the egg continues to cook in the hot saucepan. Never allow scrambled egg to get too set.
8. Pile on to hot toast and put a sprig of parsley on top (see below). Serve at once.

It is easier to wash the saucepan if you put it to soak at once in *cold* water.

As you will see, this makes a small portion suitable for breakfast. For a more generous helping use two eggs instead of one.

(left) Mixed cooked vegetables and cheese sauce (page 71)

How to vary scrambled egg

With cheese

Cook the egg as before, but when it starts to set add 25 g grated cheese.

With tomato

1. First skin the tomato by heating enough water in a saucepan to cover it.
2. When the water is boiling, put in the tomato, and leave for 1 minute only.
3. Lift it out and put into cold water.
4. When the tomato is cold, the skin will peel off easily. Cut into slices.
5. Heat the margarine in the saucepan.
6. Add the tomato and cook for 2 minutes.
7. Beat the egg with salt and pepper, but do not add any milk. Pour into the saucepan and cook as before.

With spinach. See picture, page 66.

How to poach an egg

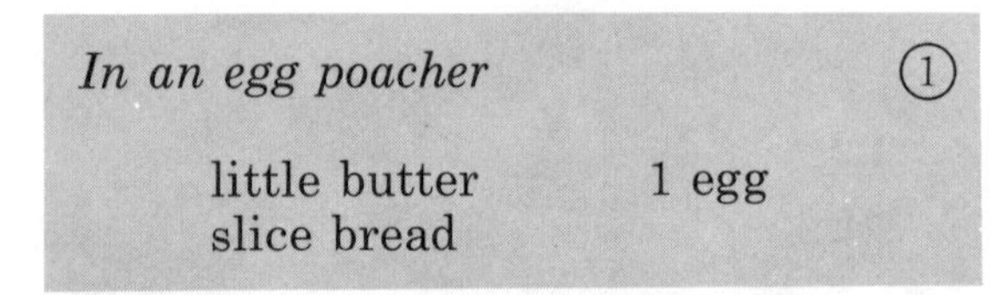

In an egg poacher ①

little butter 1 egg
slice bread

1. Warm a plate.
2. Put water in the bottom of an egg poacher. Grease one of the small metal cups with butter.
3. Heat until the water is boiling. Toast the bread, spread with butter and keep hot on a plate.
4. Break an egg into an ordinary cup. If you wet the cup first you will find the egg pours out more easily.
5. Pour into the greased metal cup and cover the poacher with a lid.
6. Cook for 2–3 minutes until the egg white sets.
7. Slide from the metal cup on to toast. Serve at once. (See picture.)

In a pan of water ①

1 slice bread	pinch salt
little butter for toast	1 egg

1. Half fill a saucepan or frying pan with water. Add a pinch of salt, and bring water to the boil. Then turn down heat so that the water boils steadily.
2. Break the egg into a wet cup, and slide it into boiling water. If you stand a greased plain round pastry cutter *in* the water, you can pour the egg into this and the white keeps a good shape. *Or* 2–3 drops of vinegar added to the water help to prevent the white from spreading.
3. Cook 2–3 minutes until the white sets.
4. If using a cutter, lift this out first. Then remove the egg with a fish slice.
5. Hold the slice and egg over the water for a few seconds to drain, so that you do not make the toast wet. Put the egg on to buttered toast and serve at once.

Other ways to serve poached egg

You can serve this on mashed potato, on cooked spinach or heated canned spaghetti (see below), or on beans in tomato sauce (see page 157). It is then a good supper meal.

What are their main nutrients?

scrambled or poached egg
poached egg served with spinach
or with baked beans or spaghetti

4. GOOD BREAKFASTS

A GOOD breakfast is an important beginning to any day. Here are ideas for breakfast from the dishes in this book.

If you do not want to cook:

Grapefruit, cereal, milk and sugar, bread or toast, butter and marmalade or honey, tea or coffee

Fruit juice, sardines and tomato, bread or

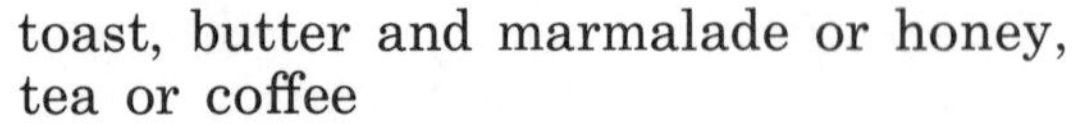

toast, butter and marmalade or honey, tea or coffee

Cheese and bread or toast and butter, fresh fruit, milk
(This meal is often served at breakfast in Scandinavian countries such as Norway and Sweden.)

With cooking:

Porridge, milk and sugar, boiled egg, bread or toast and butter, marmalade, tea or coffee.

Bacon and egg, bread or toast and butter, fresh fruit, milk, tea or coffee.

Fruit juice, bacon or sausage and tomato, milk, tea or coffee.

Cereal with milk, sugar, sliced banana, scrambled or poached egg on toast, tea or coffee.

There are many other foods you can plan for breakfast. Work out your own ideas. The picture on this page shows a new way to serve prunes. Fry bacon and tomatoes as page 53. Add cooked or well soaked strained prunes and heat in the bacon fat.

Porridge—with rolled oats

rolled oats	water
salt	

This is a quick cooking porridge: Follow the directions on the packet carefully. (See picture at right.)

Porridge—with oatmeal

③-④

50–75 g medium or coarse oatmeal (75 g gives a thicker porridge)
$\frac{1}{2}$ level teaspoon salt   840 ml water

This type of porridge takes longer to cook.

1. Put the oatmeal and salt into a basin.
2. Gradually stir in the cold water until evenly mixed. This can stand for some time. Some people like it to soak overnight.
3. Put it into a saucepan and bring to the boil, stirring all the time.
4. Lower the heat. Cook porridge made with medium oatmeal for about 45 minutes. If coarse oatmeal is used, cook for at least 1 hour. Stir from time to time to stop the porridge burning. You can prevent this if you cook the porridge in the top of a double saucepan over boiling water, but you must add 15 minutes to the cooking time.
5. Serve in warm dishes with hot or cold milk, sugar or honey, or with salt.

Setting the breakfast table

So far in this book a number of dishes have been planned for breakfast time.

You need for any breakfast table:
- cups and saucers with teaspoons
- milk jug, sugar basin
- tea or coffee pot
- toast rack, butter dish, dish for marmalade

Each person needs a plate for toast, and a small knife, together with a napkin.
The picture on page 38 shows one way of laying the table for breakfast. For this meal coffee and boiled eggs are being served, so you will need an egg-cup standing on a plate, and a small spoon.
This picture shows another setting for breakfast. Grapefruit have been halved and prepared, so a grapefruit glass or bowl standing on a plate, with a teaspoon or grapefruit spoon, is needed for each person. Cereal is also served, so you must add a dish and a dessertspoon, as well as a larger jug for milk, and extra sugar. Toast, honey and tea complete this meal.
If you plan:
- porridge, you need the same setting as for cereal;
- fruit juice, you need glasses and you generally stand them on a plate;
- bacon and egg, or bacon and sausage, a knife and fork is needed; and if this is being served to several people from a dish, then you must put a tablespoon and fork by the dish; fish such as herrings or kippers, you need a fish knife and fork.

A gay tablecloth and napkins to match are suitable for breakfast. Heatproof mats are needed under hot plates and dishes.

5. COOKING VEGETABLES

IF you cook vegetables correctly, they not only taste and look better, but keep more of their important food values.
Fresh vegetables are generally divided into three groups: root, green, pulses. When you are used to cooking those listed here, try less well-known ones.

Root vegetables

Potatoes, carrots, onions, parsnips, turnips, swedes, beetroot, celery

To prepare

Wash away soil on the outside of the vegetables in plenty of cold water.

Potatoes (picture 1)
Peel as thinly as possible, scrape when new, or scrub if cooking in skins (jackets). Halve or quarter if large, or cut into fingers. For chips, see page 159.
Carrots (picture 2)
Peel or scrape.
Parsnips, turnips (pictures 3 and 4), swedes
Peel as thinly as possible. When large, cut into halves, quarters or dice neatly.
Onions
Remove brown skin, cook whole or cut into slices or chop. Keep under water as much as possible to prevent you crying.

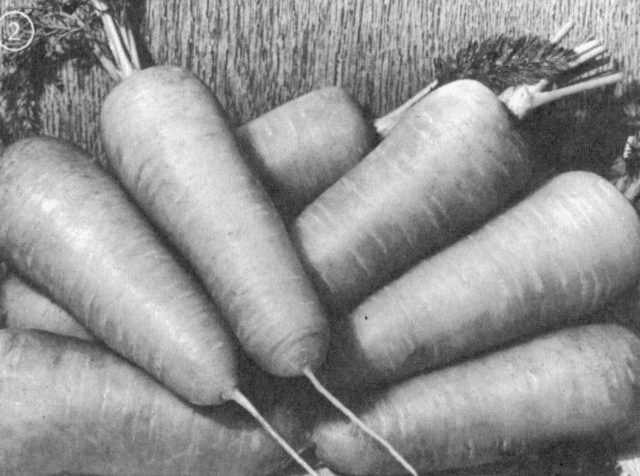
2

3

Beetroot
If raw, boil *with skin on. Do not* prick during cooking otherwise they lose colour. For ready cooked beetroot, remove the skin, slice, and serve with salad.

Celery
Remove outer green sticks; these can be chopped and used for flavouring soups or stews. Cut off the leaves, pull the other sticks away from the centre heart and wash each stick well in cold water.

To cook

The simplest way of cooking root vegetables is to boil them in salted water.

1. To each $\frac{1}{2}$ kg of *prepared* vegetables use approximately 1–1$\frac{1}{4}$ litres water and 1 *level* teaspoon salt.
2. Bring water to the boil, add salt, put in the vegetables; cover the pan with a lid. Boil *steadily*, so that the water does not boil over, until the vegetables are tender. If cooking new potatoes, put in a small sprig of washed mint.
3. The cooking time will vary, but as a guide: small old potatoes take about 20 minutes; small new potatoes 25 minutes; small carrots, turnips, parsnips, 25–30 minutes; small onions, 35–40 minutes; small raw beetroot, 1$\frac{1}{2}$–2 hours; 5 cm pieces celery, 15–20 minutes.
4. Test to see if the vegetables are tender by pressing gently with the tip of a skewer or knife.

5. *To strain,* take the pan of vegetables over to the sink, and pour the contents through a colander, standing in a bowl, to keep the vegetable water which retains vitamins from the vegetables. See page 66. If you have no colander, hold the pan firmly in your left hand, move the lid slightly away from the rim, and pour away the water. Your teacher will demonstrate this.
6. Heat 15 g butter or margarine in the saucepan and add the vegetables. Hold the saucepan over a low heat for 1 minute, to dry the vegetables.
7. Dish up and top with 2 teaspoons of chopped parsley if you like.
For other ways of cooking potatoes, see pages 71, 90, 101, 102, 158.

Green vegetables

Cabbage, Brussels sprouts, cauliflower, spinach, lettuce, watercress

To prepare

Remove the outer withered leaves. Do not waste any that are perfect. Wash them in plenty of cold water with a good pinch of salt to remove any small insects.

Cabbage, cabbage greens (pictures 5 and 6)
Put on to a chopping board and cut into fine shreds with a sharp knife.

Sprouts
Inspect carefully after washing to see they are perfect. Cut a cross with a knife at the end of each stem to make them cook evenly.

Cauliflower
Cook whole or divide into flowerets (sprigs). Cut the outer crisp stem and green leaves into smaller pieces if desired.

Spinach
Wash in several changes of cold water.

Lettuce and watercress. (See page 47.)

To cook

Green vegetables are spoilt if over-cooked or cooked in too much water.
1. To each $\frac{1}{2}$ kg of green vegetables have about 2–4 cm water in the pan.
2. Bring water to the boil, and add $\frac{1}{2}$ teaspoon salt.
3. Take the vegetables in a colander, standing on a plate, over to the cooker. Put a handful into the boiling water and let the water come back to the boil again.

Add more vegetables. In this way, you retain most vitamins in green vegetables.
4. Put on the lid and boil quickly, approximately as follows: shredded green vegetables, 5–7 minutes; sprouts, 7–10 minutes; small whole cauliflower, from 15 minutes; sprigs of cauliflower, 7–10 minutes; the green stalk of cauliflower can be put in a few minutes earlier. Spinach needs no water. After washing well, put it into a pan, with salt sprinkled lightly between each layer. Cook steadily with the lid on tightly for 15 minutes.
5. Strain as root vegetables, except that cauliflower keeps a better shape if lifted with a spoon from the pan into the colander.

Cooked cauliflower in individual scallop shells, topped with cheese sauce (page 70)

Scrambled egg on a purée of spinach (page 58)

Vegetable water

The vegetable water from cooking green vegetables is good for you, as it contains vitamins and mineral salts. Use it in gravy or for a soup; some people like to drink it. If you throw it down the sink it smells very unpleasant unless plenty of cold water is run at the same time.

The pictures on pages 63, 64, show some of the most usual vegetables. These can all be grown from seed; perhaps some of you

grow them.
(1) potatoes (2) carrots
(3) parsnips (4) turnips
There are two kinds of cabbage shown: the small cabbage, often called spring cabbage, (5) although it is planted both spring and autumn and so is available throughout most of the year, and the one with curly leaves which is a Savoy cabbage, (6).

Pulses

Peas, beans—runner, French, broad

To prepare

Peas
Pop pods between your forefinger and thumb, and remove the peas, looking for any that are not perfect. Wash.
Runner or French beans
Wash, cut off the ends and stringy sides. Use French beans whole, but cut runner beans into thin slices.
Broad beans
Remove the pods, take out the beans and wash them. When broad beans are very young, slice the pods and cook with the beans or in a separate pan.

To cook

1. To each ½ kg of *prepared* vegetables, use 1–1¼ litres water and 1 *level* teaspoon salt.
2. Cook as root vegetables. Peas need 15–20 minutes; a sprig of mint and a pinch of sugar can be added. French beans need about 20 minutes; runner beans 20–25 minutes; broad beans 15–20 minutes.

Dried vegetables

Haricot and butter beans, lentils, peas (see picture below).

To prepare and cook

1. To 100 g beans or lentils use 560 ml water and ½ teaspoon salt.

2. Bring water to the boil, pour over the beans or lentils and leave to soak overnight.
3. Put into a pan with water, add salt and simmer gently in covered saucepan until tender. For haricot beans, allow 2 hours; butter beans, 1½ hours; lentils, peas, 1 hour.
4. Strain and serve with a little margarine or butter, or in a sauce. (See pages 69–71.)

Today it is possible to buy dried peas and beans that need no soaking. This is because they are frozen and then dried. You will hear them described as A.F.D. (Accelerated Freeze Dried). Follow the directions on the packet.

Cooked frozen beans and peas

Frozen vegetables

Some of the most usual are: peas and French beans (see picture), broad beans, Brussels sprouts, mixed vegetables.
Store frozen vegetables carefully as directed on the packet. Cook for the time given on the packet. Do not over-cook as they are very young and tender.

Canned vegetables

Some of the most usual are: peas, carrots, baked beans in tomato sauce, mixed vegetables. Read the directions on the can and heat carefully.

What are their main food values?

potatoes carrots
green vegetables peas beans

6. VEGETABLES FOR A COMPLETE MEAL

ON pages 63 to 68 are some of the important things to know about cooking vegetables. Generally these are cooked and served as part of a meal; sometimes they can form the *main* part.

Either choose one vegetable, cauliflower or whole onions or butter or haricot beans or carrots, or have a selection of vegetables to make the dish more interesting and perhaps of more food value. If you serve a sauce with vegetables, a white or parsley sauce or, best of all, a cheese sauce (to provide extra protein) you will make a more nourishing meal. There are two ways of making a white sauce, which is the basis for other sauces. The first is given below and the second is on pages 151–152.

White sauce—Blending method

25 g flour	280 ml milk	②-④
pinch salt	15–25 g butter or margarine	
shake pepper		

This sauce is enough for 4 small portions or 2 large ones.

1. Mix the flour with salt and pepper in a basin.
2. Gradually add a quarter of the milk, stirring with a wooden spoon until you have a smooth paste.
3. Put the rest of the milk into a saucepan and bring to boiling point. Take care it does not boil over.

4. Pour the boiling milk slowly over the flour mixture, stirring all the time to prevent lumps forming.
5. Tip the sauce back into the pan and put over a low heat. Stir until the mixture boils, then continue cooking for 3 minutes, stirring all the time. Add the butter.
6. When stirring a sauce, make sure that the wooden spoon scrapes across the bottom and into the corners of the pan. If the sauce becomes a little lumpy, remove pan from the heat, beat the sauce with the wooden spoon, or better still with a hand whisk, until it becomes smooth.
7. Taste the sauce when cooked. If necessary, add extra salt and pepper.
8. To keep a sauce hot without a skin forming on top, cover with a round of damp greaseproof paper.

Note: After pouring out the sauce, put the pan to soak in *cold* water.

When making a white sauce to pour over vegetables, you can use half milk and half liquid in which vegetables have been cooked. This gives a very good flavour.

How to vary white sauce

Hard-boiled egg sauce, for cauliflower, boiled onions, mixed vegetables, or fish.
1. Hard boil 1 or 2 eggs. (See pages 45–46.)
2. Remove shells and chop the eggs.
3. Make the white sauce (see page 69) and, when this is cooked, add the eggs.

Mustard sauce

Blend ½–1 level teaspoon dry mustard with the flour and proceed as for blended sauce. The grilled herrings on page 127 could be served with a mustard sauce.

Cheese sauce, for cauliflower, boiled onions, boiled celery, mixed vegetables, macaroni cheese (pages 148–149), or fish.
1. Grate 50–100 g Cheddar cheese finely.
2. Make the white sauce, adding a pinch of dried mustard to the flour.
3. When the sauce is cooked, stir in the cheese.
4. Cook for 1 minute only over low heat until the cheese has melted.

Parsley sauce, to serve with beans—broad, butter or haricot, boiled onions, mixed vegetables, or with fish.

1. Chop enough washed and dried parsley to give 2–3 teaspoons.
2. Make the white sauce and, when this is cooked, add the finely chopped parsley.

Vegetables with cheese sauce

②

2 small potatoes	$\frac{1}{2}$ level teaspoon salt
2 small carrots	$\frac{1}{2}$ small cauliflower
2 small onions	280 ml cheese sauce (See page 70.)

1. Put a serving dish to warm.
2. Peel potatoes, carrots and onions.
3. Put 1–$1\frac{1}{4}$ litres water into a pan, bring to the boil, add salt and put in the vegetables.
4. Cook for 15 minutes, then add sprigs of cauliflower. Cook for a further 10 minutes.
5. Make a cheese sauce.
6. Test to see if vegetables are cooked, strain, arrange in the hot dish and cover with cheese sauce (picture, page 56).

A potato baked in its jacket (skin) is easy to cook and a very good flavour. Slit and serve it with butter.

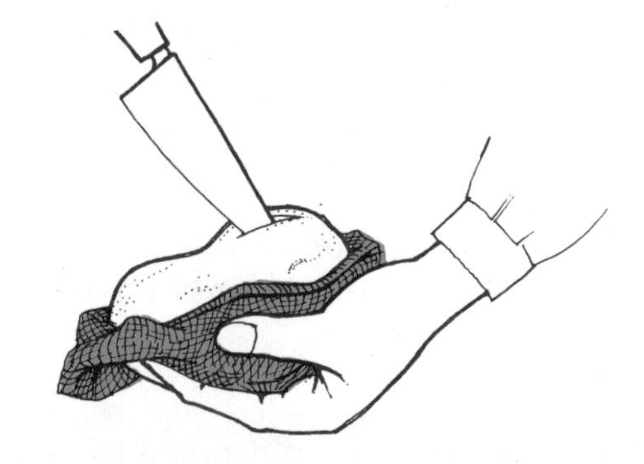

Baked potato

1 large old potato 
little butter

1. Put a plate to warm. Switch on or light the oven. (Your teacher will give you the temperature to use, for potatoes can be baked slowly or in a moderately hot oven.) Scrub the potato well, cut out any eyes, and dry.
2. Prick with a fork to prevent the skin from bursting as the potato cooks. Put on to the oven shelf, or on a baking tray.
3. Allow approximately 2 hours in a very moderate oven (160° C—Gas Mark 3), or

$1\frac{1}{4}$–$1\frac{1}{2}$ hours in a moderately hot oven (200°C — Gas Mark 6).
4. The potato is cooked when it feels soft. Lift out of the oven and put on the serving plate.
5. Make a cut on top of the potato and serve with butter. (See drawing, page 71.)

Stuffed potato

1 large old potato	pinch salt	②
50 g cheese	shake pepper	
15–25 g margarine or butter		

1. Bake the potato as above.
2. Grate the cheese.
3. Lift potato out of the oven and cut it in half. (Protect your hands with a dry tea towel.)
4. Scoop the pulp out of the potato halves with a teaspoon and put this into a basin. Keep the two halves a good shape.
5. Mash the pulp with a fork until smooth, then add the cheese, margarine, salt and pepper.
6. Put the mixture back into potato cases and return to the oven for a further 10–15 minutes.

If you like, most of the cheese can be added to the mashed potato and the rest sprinkled on top of the filled potato halves before they are reheated in the oven, and the potatoes topped with bacon rolls (page 96) and parsley (see picture).

What are their main food values?

boiled, baked or stuffed potatoes
onions, cauliflower, and the other vegetables described on pages 63 to 68
white, parsley, or cheese sauce

Bread and butter pudding (page 78

7. USING MILK

YOU will see from pages 7–8 that milk is a most important food. It is equally good whether you drink it, use it in cooking or buy it in the form of yoghourt.

Drinks with milk

Cold milk

Shake the bottle gently to distribute the cream; pour into glasses.

Hot milk

First rinse out a saucepan in cold water; this helps to prevent milk 'sticking' to the pan. Heat the milk, but do not let it boil; then pour into cups. Put the pan to soak in *cold* water after heating milk.

Chocolate—cold

glass of milk 
2 teaspoons chocolate powder

1. Pour the milk into a glass to within $2\frac{1}{2}$ cm of the top. Most glasses (tumblers) hold about 280 ml when full.
2. Add the chocolate powder and stir until dissolved. If you wish, pour your chocolate mixture into a clean tumbler.

You can serve chocolate with straws, and add a spoonful of ice-cream for special occasions, or cream and grated chocolate. (See picture below.) Chocolate powder is sweetened so no sugar is needed.

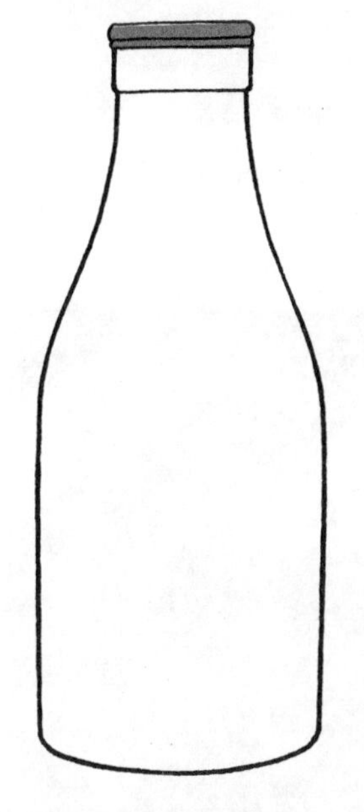

ce-cream and rose hip syrup (page 82), rose hip milk hake (page 77), rose hip syrup and soda water age 111)

Chocolate—hot

140 ml milk 2–3 teaspoons chocolate powder	①

1. Heat the milk in a saucepan.
2. Stir in chocolate and pour into a cup.

Cocoa

140 ml milk (or use half milk and half water) 1 teaspoon cocoa sugar to taste	①

1. Put the cocoa into a cup, stir in 2 tablespoons of cold milk, blend until smooth.

2. Heat the rest of the milk, pour over the cocoa, add sugar.

Some people like to pour the cocoa mixture back into the pan and heat it for one minute, then return it to the cup.

Baked rice pudding

25 g rice 15–25 g sugar	280 ml milk	②

1. Wash the rice—the kind used for milk puddings is the round or Carolina rice.
2. Grease a pie-dish and put in the rice.
3. Add the milk and sugar.
4. Bake in the coolest part of a very moderate oven (160°C—Gas Mark 3) for approximately 1 hour, or for a creamier pudding bake in a slower oven for a longer period. (120°C—Gas Mark ½ for 2 hours.)

You may like to add about 1 dessertspoon butter or suet to the rice pudding to give a richer texture.

You can put a little grated nutmeg over the top of the pudding before it is cooked.

Rice pudding can be flavoured with cocoa or chocolate; you can add a few sultanas or raisins. You can make the pudding with canned or powdered milk. (The picture above shows a milk pudding made with the latter.)

Rose hip milk shake

$\frac{3}{4}$ glass of milk 1 or 2 tablespoons rose hip syrup	①

1. Pour the milk into a basin.
2. Add the rose hip syrup.
3. Whisk together with an egg whisk.
4. Pour into the glass.

This drink adds vitamin C to milk. (See picture above.)

Canned rice pudding

To save time you can use a can of rice pudding. All you need do is to heat this in a saucepan or put it in a pie-dish, top with grated nutmeg, and cook for approximately 30 minutes in a very moderate oven (160°C—Gas Mark 3).

Bread and butter pudding

1 large slice bread	15–25 g sugar	②
15 g butter	1 egg	
15–25 g sultanas or currants	280 ml milk	

1. Butter the bread and cut into 4 triangles, fingers or squares.
2. Arrange in a pie-dish with the sultanas.
3. Put the sugar into a basin, add the egg and beat well.

4. Pour on the milk, which can be warm, stirring all the time.
5. Strain the mixture over the bread and butter. If possible, leave the pudding to stand for 15 minutes before it is baked.
6. Bake in the coolest part of a very moderate oven (160°C—Gas Mark 3) for approximately 45 minutes.

Health drinks

A number of health foods add extra goodness to milk, and some of these you may have at school or at home. Read the directions for mixing and follow them.

To make a cornflour mould

35 g cornflour	④
40–50 g sugar	
560 ml milk	
flavouring (see below)	

Use either: ½ teaspoon vanilla essence
or: 1 tablespoon coffee essence
or: 15 g cocoa

1. Tip the cornflour into a basin. For a chocolate mould, add the cocoa now.

2. Blend with a quarter of the milk until the mixture is smooth.
3. Bring the rest of the milk to the boil. This is when the vanilla or the coffee would be added.
4. Pour the milk over the cornflour mixture in the basin, stirring well.
5. Return to the saucepan with the sugar, and cook steadily over a low heat for 5 minutes, stirring all the time.
6. Rinse out a basin or mould ($\frac{1}{2}$–$\frac{3}{4}$ litre) with cold water. This makes it easier to turn out the mould.
7. Pour in the mixture. (See picture.)
8. Leave in a cold place until firmly set. If you put the mould into a refrigerator, wait until it is no longer steaming.
9. Turn out on to a plate (see picture) and serve with cream, fruit or jam.

Blancmange made with flavoured cornflour

The method of making this is exactly the same as for cornflour mould, but there is no need to add extra flavouring.

Both a cornflour mould or blancmange are richer and better tasting if you add 15 g butter at stage 5.

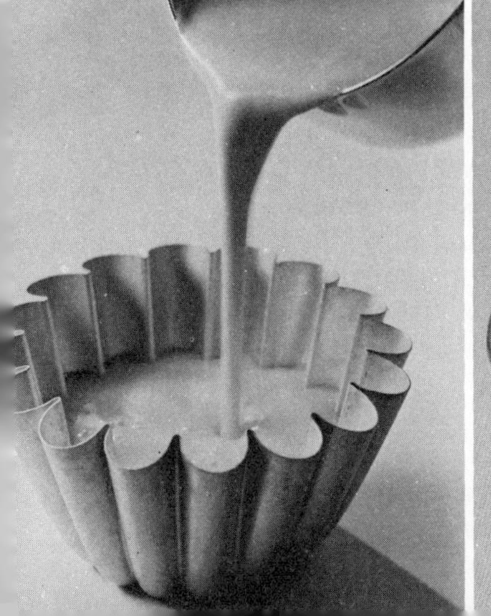

Baked custard

1 large egg	280 ml milk	②
15 g sugar		

When you cook egg and milk together, as in a bread and butter pudding or a baked custard, you must be careful that you do not use too hot an oven, or you may spoil the pudding.

When you choose the pie-dish for this pudding, also find another dish or tin; your teacher will tell you which. Put a little cold water in the dish or tin and stand the pie-dish in it.

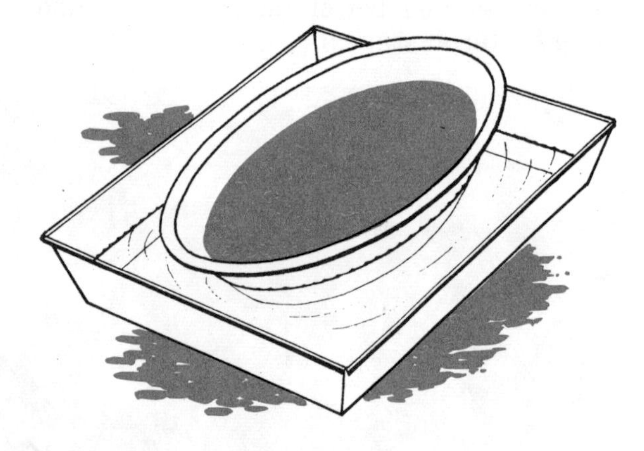

1. Break the egg into a basin.
2. Add the sugar and beat for 1 minute.
3. Pour on the milk.
4. Strain into a pie-dish and bake in the centre of a cool oven (150°C—Gas Mark 2) for approximately 45 minutes until firm.

Preserved milk

Milk can be bought in canned and powdered form. The can gives instructions on how to use this in place of fresh milk.

What nutrients are in these foods?

milk   cocoa   chocolate

a rice pudding

blancmange or cornflour mould

a bread and butter pudding or baked custard

8. QUICK PUDDINGS

THERE are many ingredients and prepared foods we can buy to make quick puddings needing little cooking. Ice-cream is a popular sweet and you can make it more interesting by adding other foods.

The picture shows chocolate sauce being poured over ice-cream—you notice the dish is not too full of ice-cream, so there is room to pour the sauce over.

Ice-cream and chocolate sauce

Individual block or portion ice-cream
Wafer biscuit

Chocolate sauce ①
15 g margarine or butter
1 *level* tablespoon cocoa
1 *level* tablespoon golden syrup
1 tablespoon water

1. Put all the ingredients for the sauce into a small pan.
2. Heat until the margarine and cocoa have quite dissolved.
3. Stand the ice-cream on a flat plate or in a grapefruit (sundae) glass.
4. Pour over the hot chocolate sauce and eat at once with the wafer. (If you prefer a cold sauce, use $1\frac{1}{2}$ tablespoons water.)

Ice-cream and rose hip syrup
Serve vanilla or strawberry ice-cream and rose hip syrup. (See picture, page 74.)

Ice-cream and fruit

small can fruit salad 
2 portions ice-cream

1. Open canned fruit.
2. Strain some of the syrup from the fruit. You can use this in a jelly.

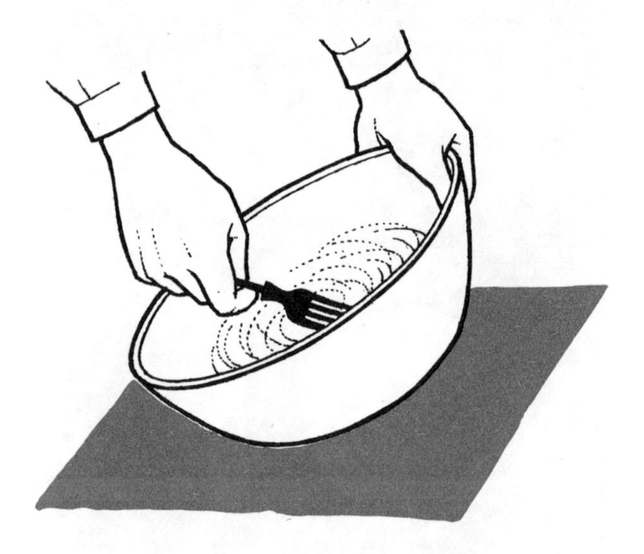

3. Arrange the fruit in 2 or 3 glasses; top with ice-cream.

Fruit and cream
Canned fruit can be served with cream. Arrange the fruit in a dish, or put it into glasses. Pour the cream into a jug or whip lightly.

To whip cream
1. Pour the cream into a clean basin.
2. Stand the basin on a folded tea towel so that it does not move as you whisk.
3. Use a hand whisk for speed, or you can whip cream with a fork.
4. The moment the cream starts to thicken, whip very slowly and carefully. If you overwhip, the cream will 'curdle'; this means it separates into hard buttery lumps and a rather watery substance.

Alternatives to cream
Fresh cream is not always obtainable and is expensive. There are alternatives to serve with fruit: custard (page 106); evaporated milk or the packet creamy topping mix, called Dream topping. (See picture, page 20.) Follow the directions for whipping on the packet.

Rice cream

Canned creamed rice makes a good cold sweet.

can creamed rice	(4)
1 small carton cream	
small can fruit	

1. Open can of rice.
2. Put the cream into a basin and whip until stiff.
3. Stir in the creamed rice and mix carefully.
4. Put into 4 grapefruit glasses or a shallow dish.
5. Strain the syrup from the fruit and arrange the fruit on top.

Packet puddings

There are several packet puddings you can buy that make a milk pudding with little cooking. One of them is shown in the picture on page 20.

Instant whip

Put 560 ml milk into a basin, add the contents of the packet and whip until dissolved. Pour into a dish and leave for 5 minutes until just firm. Serve by itself or with cream or ice-cream.

What are their food values?

ice-cream — chocolate sauce
canned fruit — cream

9. DISHES FOR SUPPER

If you want a light supper:

Sandwiches and milk or a fruit juice
Sandwich fillings are given on page 85.

Fruit juice, scrambled egg, fruit, milk.

Bread, butter, cheese and salad, milk, fresh fruit

Egg salad (see page 47), bread and butter, fresh fruit, milk

If you want a more filling supper:

Bacon, sausage, tomato, bread and butter, ice-cream and fruit, milk

Poached or fried egg with canned beans in tomato sauce, green salad, blanc-mange, fresh fruit

Vegetables with cheese sauce, ice-cream with rose hip syrup

Grapefruit, bacon and egg, bread and butter, instant whip pudding (p. 83).
Baked stuffed potatoes (p. 72), rice pudding
Sardine and egg salad (p. 48), bread and butter, stewed fruit and custard
A milk drink—cocoa, chocolate; tea or coffee may be served after supper, but where milk is given as part of the supper meal, it is because no milk has been used in cooking.
Already, as you see, you can cook enough dishes to make lots of good suppers.

Sandwiches

When you make sandwiches, cover the slices of bread with butter or margarine and add the filling. If you intend to cut the crusts off the bread, do not take the filling to the very edges. Then cover with a second slice of bread and butter. Put the sandwich on to a chopping board or bread board, remove the crusts if you wish, then cut the whole sandwich into 2 or 4.

Sandwich filling

Eggs make a good sandwich filling (see pages 46–47). Here are some others.

Ham
Use thin slices of cooked ham. You can add lettuce.

Sardine
Open a can of sardines, put into a basin and mash, adding a pinch of salt and a shake of pepper.

Cheese
Either put slices of cheese or grated cheese on the bread and butter, or spread cream cheese (picture, page 86).

Tomatoes
Skin tomatoes (see page 58), slice, put on bread and butter, add a pinch of salt and a shake of pepper.

Setting the supper table

Supper is the kind of meal where you will vary the dishes a great deal. If you have had a large tea, you will need only a light supper. For coffee and sandwiches, each person will need:

- cup, saucer, spoon
- small plate, small knife to cut sandwiches
- napkin

You will also need:
- coffee jug, milk and sugar

You may, however, plan to serve one main dish with bread and butter, then fresh fruit to follow, in which case each person will need:
- small side plate and knife
- table knife and fork
- napkin, tumbler

You will also need:
- spoon or spoon and fork to serve the dish
- serving dish for main dish
- plate for bread and butter
- bowl or plate for fruit
- water or milk jug
- salt, pepper, maybe mustard

For a supper which includes a main dish and a pudding, each person needs:
- small side plate, small knife
- table knife and fork
- dessertspoon and fork
- napkin, tumbler

You will also need:
- serving spoons
- serving dishes for main dish and sweet
- water jug
- salt, pepper, maybe mustard

Use either mats or a tablecloth, preferably with napkins to match, for supper. Remember you need heat-proof mats under hot plates and dishes, unless the table is covered with laminated plastic.

White bread, cheese and lettuce sandwiches

10. ROASTING MEAT

WHEN meat is to be roasted you should choose a good quality joint, as tougher pieces need very slow cooking by stewing. The word 'roasting' is used to describe the cooking of meat in an oven, but some people prefer to call this baking, and say roasting meat should be done on a spit. Many modern cookers have spits under the grill or in the oven.

Choosing the meat for roasting or baking

Buy by weight.
These are the joints:

Beef
topside, rib, sirloin, thick rump

Mutton or *Lamb*
loin, best end of neck, breast, leg, shoulder, (You can buy half a leg or half a shoulder.)

Pork
loin, leg, shoulder, blade-bone (You can buy half a leg or half a shoulder.)

Veal
loin, best end of neck, breast, leg, shoulder (You can buy half a leg or half a shoulder.)

Planning the meal

Certain foods are generally served with each kind of meat in addition to potatoes and green vegetables. You may not prepare them the first time you cook the joint, but they are given in this chapter.

Beef
Yorkshire pudding, horseradish sauce, mustard, gravy

Mutton
onion sauce or red currant jelly, gravy

Lamb
mint sauce—in summer time serve new potatoes and fresh peas, gravy

Pork
sage and onion stuffing, apple sauce, gravy

Veal
bacon rolls, gravy, sometimes stuffing

To prepare for roasting

1. If meat has been frozen, let it thaw out slowly. Put it on a large plate or dish.
2. Wipe meat with kitchen paper or muslin. Page 206 tells about storing meat.
3. Weigh meat to work out the cooking time. If stuffed, weigh *after* stuffing.

You may be given a very small joint, about ½ kg, to cook in class, but when you plan your own meals remember that a large piece has a better flavour. About 1¼–1½ kg is the smallest joint to give a reasonable size; any left can be served cold with salad.

Cooking times

	per ½ kg.	extra time
Beef	15-20 minutes (15 minutes for underdone beef)	15-20 minutes
Lamb	20 minutes	20 minutes
Mutton	25 minutes	25 minutes
Pork or veal	25 minutes	25 minutes

These times are suitable for most joints. If you get a very thick joint, it does take a little longer for the heat to penetrate, so add another 10 minutes.
If you are using a covered roasting tin, or wrapping the meat in foil, you must allow longer. (See page 89.)
It is quite easy to work out the times.
A ½ kg joint of beef would take:
20 minutes plus 20 minutes extra, i.e. 40 minutes.
A 1½ kg joint of mutton would take:
3 times 25 minutes, i.e. 75 minutes, plus the 25 minutes extra time, which makes a total of 1 hour 40 minutes.
This is for roasting in a *hot* oven; but some people prefer to cook meat more slowly, for a longer time. Your teacher will tell you about this.

To roast or bake meat in the oven

joint meat fat

1. Light or switch on the oven. Set to hot (220°C—Gas Mark 7).
2. Put the meat into the tin.
3. If you are roasting potatoes with the

meat, add 50 g fat or dripping. If you are *not* roasting potatoes with the meat, then add only about 25 g fat to a $\frac{1}{2}$ to 1 kg joint of lean beef and a little less with lamb. Mutton or pork, because it has quite a lot of its own fat, requires none added, but to give crisp crackling to pork, rub skin or fat with small amount of oil, melted butter or lard, or coarse salt.

4. Cook meat for the first 15 minutes at the high temperature, putting the meat in a hot part of the oven. Then lower heat to moderately hot for the rest of the time (190–200°C—Gas Mark 5–6).
5. Add potatoes during cooking. (See page 90.)
6. When meat and potatoes are cooked, put on to a hot dish while you finish making the gravy. (See page 9.)

Note: If roasting on a spit, then allow the same cooking time and follow the cooker instructions.

If roasting or baking in a covered *tin,* allow 10 minutes extra time on a joint up to $1\frac{1}{2}$ kg in weight. A covered tin is not good for browning potatoes. If roasting or baking in *foil*, allow 15 minutes extra time or 1 mark or 10°C higher on the oven setting.

Both these methods keep the oven very clean and the meat moist.

In order to brown the outside of meat when cooked in foil, open the foil for the last 20 minutes of the cooking time. (See picture, page 91.)

To lift meat from the roasting tin

1. Bring the tin out of the oven using oven gloves.
2. Stand on an asbestos mat or large pan stand on a table or flat surface.
3. Put the hot meat dish beside the tin.
4. Either lift from the tin with a fish slice under the meat and a fork to support it, or with 2 forks pushed into the meat on either side.

To roast potatoes

about ½ kg potatoes
50 g fat

1. Peel potatoes, wash and dry thoroughly.
2. Small potatoes can be roasted whole; larger potatoes should be cut up.
3. These will take about 50 minutes to cook, so work out the time they need to go into the oven. E.g. if the meat needs 1 hour 20 minutes cooking, then the potatoes are added to the tin after the meat has been cooking for 30 minutes.
4. If preferred, roast potatoes in a separate tin. To do this, get fat really hot in the oven. This takes nearly 10 minutes.
5. When potatoes go into hot fat in the meat or another tin, roll them round with two spoons or a fork and spoon so that they are coated with fat. They can be turned once *during* cooking.
6. When cooked, lift out with a fish slice to make sure they are not greasy.

To make gravy

If you have bones sent with the meat, i.e. boned sirloin of beef, breast of lamb, wash these, then simmer with 560 ml water to make stock.

If you have no bone stock for gravy you can use vegetable water *or* use water and a stock cube, yeast extract or gravy powder.

1. When the meat is cooked, pour off all the fat except for 1 tablespoon. (Do not waste this fat; put it into a basin for dripping.)
2. You will probably find there is a brown sediment at the bottom of the tin. This comes from the meat and helps to give a good flavour to the gravy, so keep this.
3. *For a thin gravy:* measure out 280 ml stock. Blend 1 level tablespoon flour with about ¼ of this to a smooth paste.

Topside of beef cooked in foil

4. Add the rest of the stock.
5. Pour into the meat tin and put on the top of the cooker over moderate heat. Bring to the boil, stirring all the time, and boil until the mixture thickens slightly.
6. Turn the heat down very low and simmer for 3–4 minutes.
7. *For a thick gravy:* 280 ml stock and 25 g flour. Do not use any more.
8. When the gravy is cooked, pour through a strainer into a sauce-boat.

Note: Some people like to use cornflour instead of flour. Use half quantity.

A thin gravy is generally served with meats that are not stuffed, and a thick gravy with stuffed meats, although most people prefer a thickened gravy with mutton.

Instead of making gravy in the meat roasting tin, you can make it in a saucepan. Pour off any extra fat into a bowl, then spoon the remaining fat and sediment into a saucepan and make gravy as above.

To serve with beef

Yorkshire pudding

horseradish sauce mustard

(Left) Grilled cutlets of New Zealand lamb and tomatoes (page 98). (Right) Roast leg of lamb

Yorkshire pudding

batter mixture (page 180) 
made with 100 g flour, etc.
25 g fat or dripping

1. Make the batter as on page 180.
2. Put the fat into the Yorkshire pudding tin, or divide this between small patty tins. You can make either one large pudding or small ones.
3. Work out the time to put this in the oven. To heat the fat and cook a large pudding takes about 35–40 minutes. To heat the fat and cook small puddings takes about 20 minutes.
4. Put the fat into the oven for 5 minutes.
5. Pour in the batter and put back into the hottest part of the oven.
6. Dish up *after* the meat and potatoes so that it keeps crisp. Cut a large pudding into neat pieces.

Horseradish sauce (or cream) is generally purchased ready made today, as it keeps well. To grate fresh horseradish, which looks rather like parsnip, takes a long time.

To make mustard

2–3 teaspoons mustard 
1 tablespoon water or milk

1. Put the mustard into a basin.
2. Gradually stir in the water or milk, blending until smooth.
3. Mustard made with milk does not harden so easily as when made with water.

To serve with mutton

Onion sauce

2 medium onions	140 ml milk	(4)
$\frac{1}{2}$ teaspoon salt	15–25 g butter or margarine	
25 g flour	pepper	

1. Peel and chop the onions finely.
2. Put into a saucepan with 280 ml water and salt.
3. Cover pan, and cook the onions for about 20 minutes.
4. Blend the flour with the milk in a basin as in blending sauce. (Page 69.)

5. Add to the cooked onions with the butter or margarine.
6. Bring to the boil and cook steadily, stirring all the time, for 3–4 minutes. Add a shake of pepper.
7. Pour carefully into a sauce-boat.

Red currant jelly. You can buy a jar of this ready made.

To serve with lamb

Mint sauce

2 heaped tablespoons mint leaves (4)
2 teaspoons sugar
½ tablespoon hot water
2 tablespoons vinegar

1. Wash and dry the mint leaves.
2. Put on to a chopping board with 1 teaspoon sugar. (This helps to chop the mint finely.)
3. Chop until fine, then put into a sauce-boat.
4. Add the rest of the sugar, stir in the hot water and leave for a few minutes to dissolve sugar.
5. Add the vinegar.

To serve with pork

Sage and onion stuffing

Either make up packet stuffing or use this recipe:

2 large onions (4)
¼ teaspoon salt, 25 g suet
50 g breadcrumbs (page 179)
1 teaspoon powdered sage
pinch pepper, 1 egg

1. Peel the onions.
2. Put on to a chopping board, cut first into slices, then chop finely.
3. Put into a saucepan with the salt and 140 ml water. Cover the pan tightly and cook steadily for 15 minutes.
4. Strain water from the onions and save this to use a little in the stuffing. The rest of the water could be added to the gravy.
5. Add the rest of the ingredients and about a tablespoon onion stock.
6. Either bake in a separate dish from the meat for 30 minutes, or your teacher will show you how to slit the meat and put in the stuffing.

Roast pork with stuffing (page 95)

Apple sauce

Make this like the fruit purée on pages 104–105. When cooked, the mixture could be sieved then reheated.

To serve with veal

Bacon rolls

rashers streaky bacon

Cut the rinds off the bacon and divide each rasher into 2 or 3.
Roll firmly and push on to metal skewers.
Stand the rolls on a tin or ovenproof plate.
Put into the oven for the last 10–15 minutes when roasting veal.

Dripping from meat

When meat has been roasted the fat that comes from it, called dripping, is put into a basin to use in cooking. Sometimes there are pieces of fat that are cut away from meat before it is cooked. If these are put into a tin in the oven, and heated until crisp you will obtain more useful dripping. To keep dripping fresh, it should be cleared regularly.

Dripping

To clear dripping, generally known as 'cleaning' or 'clarifying'.
Dripping contains tiny pieces (particles) of food. These, like all foods, will go bad in time and spoil the dripping. But if you clear the dripping you remove the particles, and it will keep until you need it again.

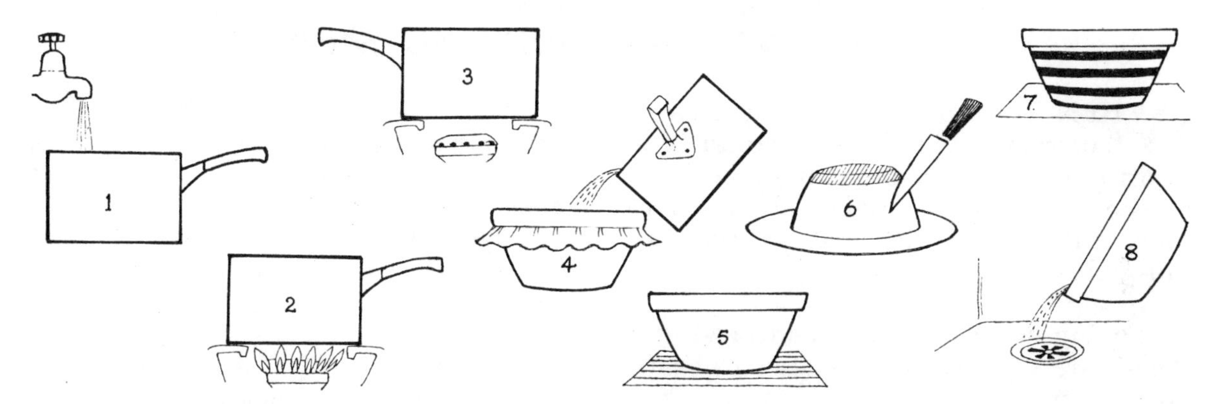

1. Put the dripping into a large saucepan and cover with cold water.
2. Bring slowly to the boil and then boil steadily for 20 minutes.
Do not have the heat very high, otherwise the dripping and water could boil over.
3. After 20 minutes, allow the dripping to cool slightly.
4. Put a thick piece of muslin or a fine sieve over a basin, hold the saucepan firmly and pour dripping and water slowly through into the basin.
5. Allow to stand until the dripping is solid again.
6. Lift the dripping away from the water and turn it upside down. You will find a brown layer at the bottom. Scrape this away. It can be used in gravy, but must not be kept with the dripping.
7. Put the clear dripping in a basin, in a cool place.
8. The tiny particles of food will have been dissolved in the water, which is then thrown away.

What are their main nutrients?

roast meat and gravy
Yorkshire pudding
roast potatoes.

11. FRYING AND GRILLING MEAT

WHEN frying or grilling meat, choose tender cuts that will be cooked in a short time. In frying or grilling, the meat is cooked quickly to seal in the flavour, then the heat is lowered to cook it through to the middle.

Choosing meat for grilling and frying

These are some of the most usual meats to grill or fry:

Beef
steak (the most popular being fillet or rump steak, both of which are very expensive)

Lamb
chops, cutlets (the fat is trimmed away from the bottom of the chop bone to give a cutlet)

Pork
chops

Veal
chops; slices of veal from the leg often given the name ' escallop '

Liver
calf's, lamb's or pig's liver cut in slices

Bacon
thin or thick streaky or back rashers; thick gammon rashers

Sausages
(see page 54.)

Note. Mutton is not suitable for quick cooking.

To grill meat

1. Wipe meat as for roasting.
2. Switch on or light the grill for about 5 minutes before putting the meat under, except for bacon, which is better put under the grill before the grill is heated. This stops bacon curling badly.
3. Brush lean meats—steak, veal, liver, lean part of lamb, thick gammon (bacon) rashers—with a little melted butter or fat. Stand on the metal or wire grid of the grill pan.
4. Cook quickly on the top side for the time given in the table. Turn the meat over with two knives or tongs, but do not put a fork into it, or the juices will run out and you lose some of the flavour.

·illed rump steak with tomatoes and mushrooms

5. Brush again with melted fat; cook quickly on the second side. Lower heat and, if necessary, move the grill pan further away from heat. Cook more slowly through to the centre. Thin rashers of bacon do not need turning.
6. If cooking tomatoes with the meat, either put them into the grill pan under the grid, or add them towards the end of the cooking time.
7. Arrange on a hot plate or serving dish.

Times for grilling or frying meat

	on high heat for 1st side	for second side	with lowered heat
Beef (steaks) —time will vary with thickness	2-3 minutes	2 minutes	2 minutes for underdone; 4-6 minutes medium; 6-10 minutes well done.
Lamb chops	3-4 minutes	3-4 minutes	6-8 minutes
Pork chops	5 minutes	5 minutes	10 minutes
Veal	5 minutes	5 minutes	10 minutes
Bacon— thin rashers	3-5 minutes	no need to turn	no need to lower heat
thick rashers	3-4 minutes	3-4 minutes	6-8 minutes
Liver— slices (better fried)	2-3 minutes	2-3 minutes	2-3 minutes
Sausages— depends on size	4-5 minutes	4-5 minutes	5-6 minutes

To grill bacon and sausages

1–2 rashers bacon	1–2 sausages ①
1 tomato	

1. Put plate or dish to warm.
2. Prick sausages, put on to grid of grill pan and put under hot grill.
3. Cook for 8–10 minutes, then add rasher of bacon and tomato halves, and finish cooking.
4. Serve with mustard. You do not need gravy.

Note: When grilling a lot of bacon and sausages you may not have room for both on the pan, so cook the sausages first, put on hot dish and keep warm. Then cook the bacon.

To fry meat

In frying meat, as in frying other foods, remember to watch the heat carefully. You need a high heat to seal both sides of meat, then a lower heat to cook the meat through to the middle without browning.

1. Wipe meat as for roasting. Put a serving plate or dish to warm, with an extra plate or tin for draining. (See point 5.)
2. With lean meat—steak, veal, liver, lean lamb or very lean gammon rashers (bacon)—put 25 g fat or dripping into the frying pan. Pork, unless very lean, needs no fat; sausages and thin bacon rashers need no fat. (See pages 53–54.)
3. Heat the fat until just a faint haze is seen, or a cube of bread turns golden brown in 1 minute. Put in the meat (coat liver with flour, see page 101) and cook for the time given. Turn over with two knives or tongs, but do not put a fork into meat; juices run out and flavour is lost.
4. Cook quickly on the second side, then turn heat down very low and finish cooking. Halved tomatoes can be added for the last 4 minutes of cooking time.
5. Put a piece of kitchen paper or crumpled tissue paper on the spare plate or tin.
6. Lift meat on to the paper and leave for 1 minute so that the fat drains away.
7. Arrange on serving plate or dish.
8. You can make gravy if you wish. (See pages 90, 93 and 102.)
9. You will be told if you are to strain the fat from the pan for further use.

To fry liver

50–75 g liver $\frac{1}{2}$ level tablespoon flour pinch salt shake pepper 25 g fat 1 rasher bacon	①

1. Place a serving plate to warm.
2. Put the flour on to a plate or piece of greaseproof paper with salt and pepper. Cut rind from the bacon.
3. Wipe liver and press each slice into the flour until covered. This is called 'coating'. Shake any extra flour off the liver back on to the plate or paper.
4. Heat the fat and cook the liver for 2–3 minutes, then turn it over and cook for 1 minute.
5. Add the rasher of bacon. A halved tomato can also be put in the pan. Finish cooking. (See picture.)
6. There is no need to drain fried liver on paper like other meats; it should not be greasy.

To serve with fried or grilled meats

Creamed or mashed potatoes

$\frac{1}{2}$ kg potatoes 15–25 g margarine 2 tablespoons milk	pinch salt shake pepper	④

1. Prepare the potatoes and cook until soft. (See pages 63–65.)
2. Strain and return to the saucepan.
3. Break into fine pieces, this is called

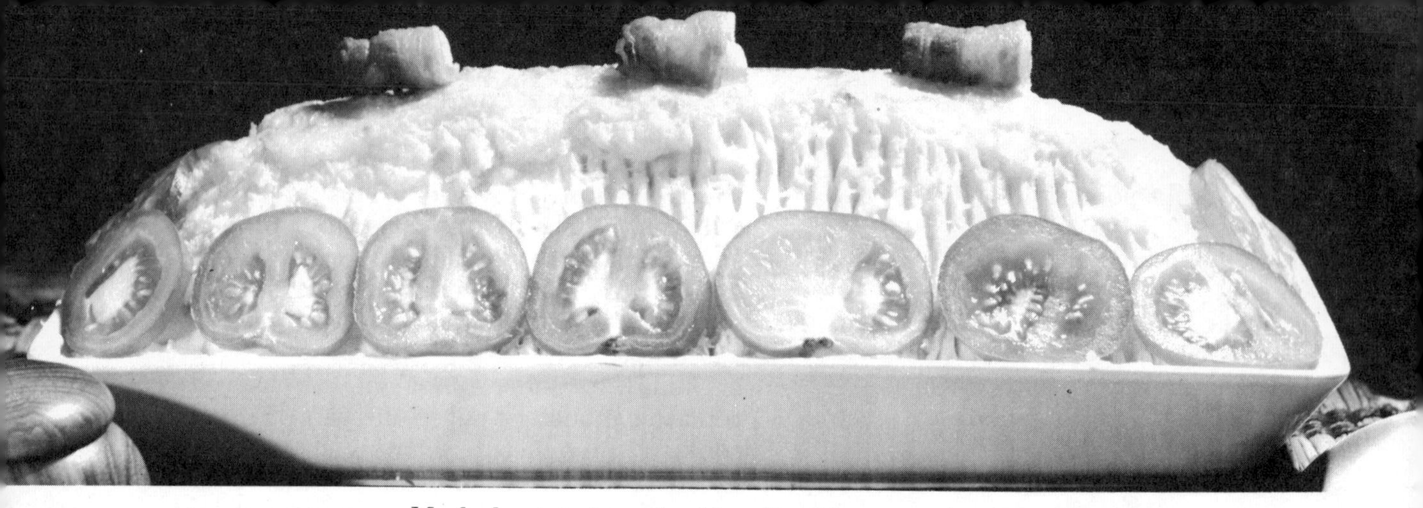

Mashed potato topped with rolls of bacon and garnished with slices of tomato. The mashed potato has been given extra flavour by adding a little grated cheese

'mashing', with a fork or potato masher.
4. Add the margarine, milk, salt and pepper.
5. Beat hard with the fork or a wooden spoon until soft and smooth.
6. Pile into a hot serving dish, making a neat shape; mark with a fork.

Making gravy for fried or grilled meats

If you wish to make gravy either:

1. Pour out all the fat from the frying pan except 1 tablespoon, *or*
2. Pour 1 tablespoon fat from the grill pan into the saucepan.

Make gravy as on pages 90 and 93.

A frying pan or grill pan is easier to wash up if first cleaned with kitchen paper.

What food values are in fried and grilled meats?

12. FRUIT IN PUDDINGS

WE are fortunate in this country in having a good variety of fruits throughout the year and these recipes are suitable for most fruits.

Stewed fruit

½ kg fruit (4)
140 ml water with juicy ripe fruit
280 ml water with hard or firm fruit
50–75 g sugar

1. Prepare the fruit. Peel apples very thinly, cut into quarters, remove core, then slice neatly. To keep them a good colour, place in a covered container as you prepare them. Halve apricots and large plums; remove stones and wash in cold water. 'Top and tail', that is cut both ends from, gooseberries and wash in cold water. Wash black and red currants. Wash rhubarb and cut into neat pieces.
2. Put water and sugar into a large saucepan; heat gently until the sugar dissolves.
3. Add fruit and put a lid on the pan.

4. Simmer *very slowly* until fruit is tender but unbroken. Soft fruits take about 10 minutes; hard fruits about 20 minutes.
5. If serving hot, pour into a warmed dish, or allow to cool in the pan. Then arrange in a serving dish.

Oven-cooked fruit

Fruit may be cooked in a casserole in the oven, with water and sugar. Cover and cook fresh fruit for 15–30 minutes, dried fruit for $1\frac{1}{4}$ hours, in a very moderate oven (160°C—Gas Mark 3).

Stewed dried fruit

200 g dried fruit	25–50 g sugar ④
280 ml water	

1. Wash the dried prunes, apricots or figs.
2. Put into a basin, add the cold water; leave soaking overnight.
3. Pour water and fruit into a saucepan; add the sugar.
4. Put a lid on the pan and simmer very slowly for about 1 hour until tender. Use 420 ml water if you want more juice. A tablespoon of lemon juice can be added.

Some recipes need the fruit cooked to a thick purée or pulp. To obtain approximately 280 ml purée you need:

Fruit purée

200 g prepared fruit ②
4 tablespoons water with
  juicy ripe fruit
8 tablespoons water with
  hard firm fruit
25–40 g sugar

Prunes and grapefruit for breakfast

1. Put all the ingredients into a saucepan over very low heat.
2. Cook, stirring often, until a smooth thick mixture is obtained.
3. Rub through a sieve if necessary.

Fruit snow

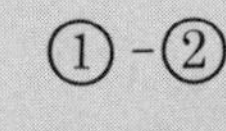

140 ml fruit purée
1 egg white

1. Let the fruit purée become quite cold.
2. Separate the egg white from the yolk. Your teacher will show you how to do this by cracking the egg and allowing the white to drop into one basin and the yolk into another. Another way is to break the egg carefully on to a plate. Then put an egg-cup over the yolk and pour the white into a basin.
3. Stand the basin on a folded tea towel to keep it steady and use a hand or rotary whisk to whip the egg white until it is very stiff. The egg yolk could be added to a custard. (See pages 106–107.)
4. Add the white to the fruit purée and fold together.
5. Put into glasses or a serving dish.
6. Decorate with a *small piece* of glacé cherry or angelica. (See picture, page 109.)

Fruit salad

②-③

1 small can fruit
(apricots or pineapple or peaches)
few grapes
1 large orange
1 banana
1 eating apple
1 ripe pear

There are many ways of making a fruit salad. The easiest is to use canned *and* fresh fruit together.

1. Open the can of fruit and pour the syrup into a basin. Put the fruit on a plate and cut into neat pieces; add to syrup.
2. Halve grapes, remove pips. Peel the orange, take out segments of fruit and remove skin and pips.
3. Peel banana, apple and pear and cut into neat pieces. Do this just before serving so that they keep a good colour.
4. Mix with the canned fruit and syrup; put into serving dish.

Baked apple

1 cooking apple 

1. Wash and dry the apple.
2. Remove the centre core with apple corer or potato peeler. Stand in oven-proof baking dish.
3. Slit the skin round centre with tip of a sharp knife to prevent it bursting in cooking.
4. The apple can be cooked in a very moderate oven (160°C—Gas Mark 3). Allow 50 minutes–1 hour for small to medium apples, 1–1¼ hours for large apples; or cook for approximately 35–40 minutes for small to medium, 40–50 minutes for medium to large apples in a moderately hot oven (190–200°C—Gas Mark 5–6).

The centre can be filled before baking with:

1. 2 teaspoons dried fruit, 2 teaspoons sugar
2. 15 g butter, 2 teaspoons brown sugar
3. 1 tablespoon bramble jelly
4. 1 tablespoon golden syrup

Custard sauce

The most usual sauce to serve with fruit is custard. If using custard powder, it is made in the same way as a cornflour mould. (See pages 78–79.)

For a pouring sauce

1 level tablespoon custard powder ④
280 ml milk
15–25 g sugar

For a thick sauce for the fruit fool

2 level tablespoons custard powder ④
280 ml milk
15–25 g sugar

1. Put the custard powder into a basin.
2. Blend with 4 tablespoons cold milk.
3. Bring rest of milk to the boil in a pan, rinsed out first in cold water.
4. Pour on to custard powder and cold milk, stirring well.
5. Return mixture to saucepan, add sugar and bring to the boil. Cook slowly, stirring well, for 3 minutes.

If you wish to use up the left-over egg yolk, beat this with 2 tablespoons milk and strain into the custard when thickened at stage 5. Heat *without* boiling for 1 minute.
The picture shows boiling milk being poured over blended custard. For convenience the basin is on top of the cooker—the milk was boiled on one of the back hot plates.

Never stand mixing basins on warm plates on the cooker.

Fruit fool

280 ml thick custard 
280 ml fruit purée

1. Spoon the custard into a fairly large mixing bowl.
2. Let it cool slightly, then stir in the *cool* fruit purée.
3. Beat the custard and fruit very hard with a wooden spoon.
4. Put either into 4 grapefruit (sundae) glasses or a serving dish.
5. When the mixture is very cold, decorate with a small piece of cherry or angelica if you wish. (See picture, page 109.)

What are their food values?

fresh fruit salad	cooked dried fruits
cooked fresh fruits	custard

13. FRUIT DRINKS

FRESH fruit or fruit syrup make delicious cold or hot drinks.

Quick lemonade

1 lemon 2 teaspoons sugar (you can use more.) water	①

1. Squeeze the juice from 1 lemon.
2. Put it with the sugar into a glass.
3. Add hot or cold water.

Economical lemonade

This takes the flavour from the peel as well as from the juice.

2 large lemons 1–2 tablespoons sugar 700 ml boiling water	④

1. Squeeze the juice out of the lemons and put into a jug.
2. Put the peel into a large jug and add the sugar.
3. Pour over the boiling water.
4. Let this water cool and, as it cools, press the lemon halves hard to get out as much flavour as possible.
5. Strain into a clean jug and add the lemon juice.

Instead of putting the lemon halves into a jug, they can be put into a saucepan with the sugar and 840 ml cold water. Bring the water to the boil and simmer for 5 minutes. Cool and strain into a jug; add the lemon juice.

Fruit fool (page 107) and fruit snow (page 10

Orangeade

Use either of the recipes for lemonade, but you may not need as much sugar.

Rose hip drink

1–2 tablespoons rose hip syrup 
water or soda water

1. Put the syrup into a glass.
2. Fill up with hot or cold water, or with soda water. (See picture, page 74.)

Black currant drink

1–2 tablespoons black currant syrup
water or soda water ①

1. Put the syrup into a glass.
2. Fill up with hot or cold water, or with soda water.

Raw fruit

No pudding is better for you or more delicious than fresh fruit.

If you are eating the peel of fruit, wash this carefully, for it has been handled a great deal.

(Above) Several kinds of fresh fruit: orange, pear, apple, tangerine, peaches, grapes, plums (Left) Baked apples stuffed with sultanas (page 106), stewed apples and custard (pages 103 and 106)

14. FOR DINNER

As this is the main meal of the day, plan it carefully so that it is good to eat and the flavours go well together. Here are dinners based on some of the dishes in the first part of this book:

Roast beef, roast potatoes, gravy, cabbage; oven-cooked fruit and ice-cream

Fried liver and bacon, mashed potatoes, peas; fruit fool

Cold meat, jacket potatoes, salad; rice pudding

Grilled sausages and tomatoes, mashed potatoes; stewed fruit and custard

Vegetables and cheese sauce; fruit snow

Roast lamb, roast potatoes, gravy, cauliflower; blancmange

Oven-cooked sausages, tomatoes, jacket potatoes; baked apples

Oven-cooked sausages

sausages
very little fat

1. Prick the sausages.
2. Grease the tin and put in the sausages.
3. Cook large sausages for 30 minutes, smaller sausages for 20 minutes in the hottest part of a moderately hot oven (190–200°C—Gas Mark 5–6) *or* allow 35–40 minutes for small sausages and 40–45 minutes for large sausages in a moderate oven (180°C—Gas Mark 4), until brown. Turn them over with a fish slice half-way through cooking.
4. Halved tomatoes may be put into the tin for the last 10 minutes.

Setting the dinner table

Each person needs:

- table knife and fork
- dessert spoon and fork
- small knife
- glass for water
- side plate and napkin

There are two ways in which these can be laid:

(1) The small knife inside on the right, then the dessert spoon, then the large knife. The small dessert fork inside on

left, and large table fork outside. The glass at the right; the side plate and napkin at the left.

(2) Put the large fork, small knife and large knife as before. Put the dessert fork across the top with the prongs pointing to the knives, the dessert spoon on top with the bowl towards the fork. The glass and napkin as in (1).

If you plan:

Soup Set a soup spoon *outside* the large knife.

Fish Use a fish knife and fork instead of a table knife and fork.

Grapefruit Either put a small spoon on the plate with the grapefruit glass or across the top of the fork and knife.

You will also need to set:

Serving spoons, generally put at the corners of the table

Salt, pepper and probably mustard

Carving knife and fork, laid on each side of the meat dish

If the gravy boat does not pour, a spoon is needed to serve the gravy

Water jug

Dishes and plates for meat, vegetables and pudding

Use mats or a tablecloth for dinner. Remember that you need heatproof mats under hot plates and dishes unless the table is covered with laminated plastic.

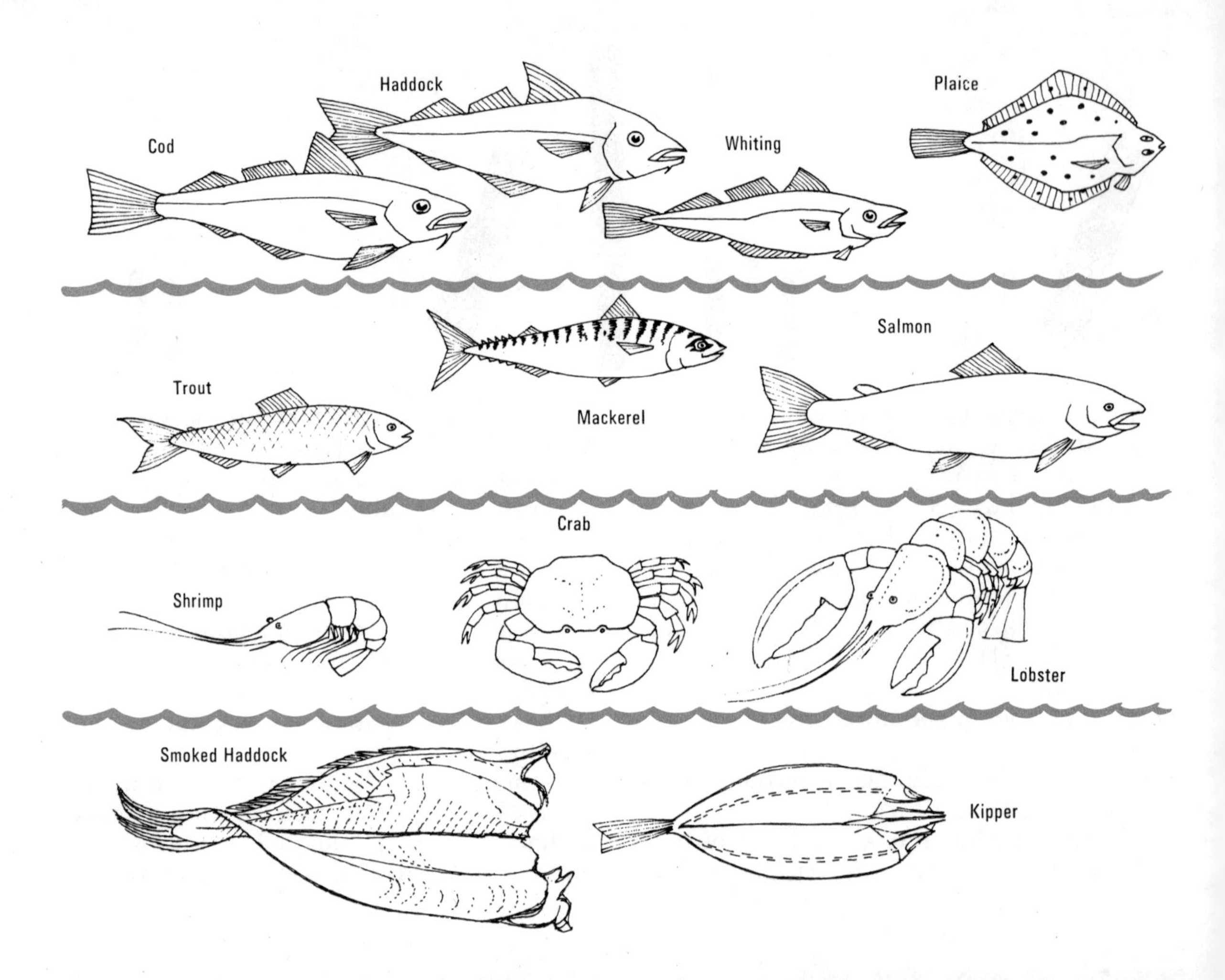
Haddock
Plaice
Cod
Whiting
Salmon
Trout
Mackerel
Crab
Shrimp
Lobster
Smoked Haddock
Kipper

15. COOKING FISH

FISH is an important protein food, and you can cook it in many ways to make interesting dishes. Because it is easy to digest, fish is a good food to serve for evening meals, and when people are ill. *When you buy fish* shop wisely, for it spoils easily, particularly in hot weather. Store carefully; you can read more about this on page 207.
Do not over-cook fish, whichever method you use, for you will make it dry and tasteless. You can test to see if the fish is cooked by pressing gently with the tip of a knife. The fish flakes should just come away from each other or from the skin or bone, and the flesh will look very white. Serve fish as quickly as possible after cooking.
Fish is put under four groups.

White fish
There are many kinds: cod, haddock, hake, whiting, rock salmon are some of the most economical; plaice and sole are more expensive.

Oily fish
This includes herrings, and herrings treated to become kippers or bloaters; mackerel and sprats; these are cheap and very good food value. Salmon is also an oily fish but an expensive one.

Shellfish
Prawns, shrimps, crabs, lobsters are some of the most usual; they are usually sold ready cooked by fishmongers.

Smoked fish
White fish such as cod and haddock are smoked and make good breakfast or supper dishes. Herrings are split and smoked in a special way to become kippers.

Always wash your hands *after* as well as *before* handling fish. A teaspoon of dry mustard rubbed on before washing removes any fish smell. When cooking fish, keep the windows open where convenient and wash up used pans as soon as possible.

You may need to skin or fillet fish before cooking. It is useful to know how to do this yourself, although most fishmongers will do it for you. Later on you will learn how to fillet and skin fish.

To cook white fish

White fish can be cooked in many ways. Here are the more important:
Poached, cooked in water
Fried, cooked in fat
Grilled, cooked under the grill
Baked, cooked in the oven
Steamed, cooked *over* water

To poach white fish

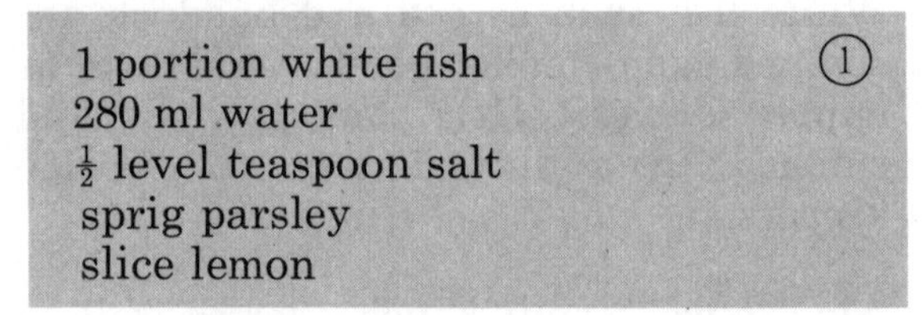

1 portion white fish ①
280 ml water
½ level teaspoon salt
sprig parsley
slice lemon

(This fish can be a piece of large fillet, steak or cutlet—slice of cod, haddock, etc.—or a whole fillet of plaice and even a small whole plaice or whiting.)

1. Wash the fish in cold water.
2. Pat dry on kitchen paper.
3. Put a plate to warm.
4. Put the water, salt and fish into a wide shallow saucepan. Some people use a deep frying pan. It is important to keep the fish flat so that it does not break; cover the pan with a lid if possible.
5. Bring water to the boil, turn down heat and *simmer* for 3 minutes for thin fillet of plaice, 5 minutes for thicker fillet of cod or haddock, 7 minutes for *thick* steak of haddock, cod or whole fish. Test before removing from the water to see if it is cooked.

6. Lift fish out of liquid with a fish slice. Hold this over the pan for 1 minute, allowing the fish to drain, then put the fish on to the warm plate.
7. Pour water away and rinse the pan in plenty of cold water before washing.

Poached fish *looks* dull, so add colour with a sprig of parsley and a slice of lemon or halved tomato. Or why not serve it with a cheese or white sauce? (See pages 69–70, 151–152. Picture, page 128.)
Serve poached fish with mashed potatoes, pages, 101–102. Peas or cauliflower are good vegetables to serve with the fish.

Fried white fish

This is the most popular way of serving fish. It is good because it keeps in most of the flavour, and fried fish looks attractive.
Frying is *not* an easy way of cooking—you will probably have read about it before, when frying meat. If not, read page 100 now, for fish is easily spoiled by *bad* frying.
In order to give a good colour to the outside of the fish and to prevent it from breaking, it is first coated. You can coat with egg and crumbs or batter. (You will learn about these later.) The easiest coating is flour.

Frying a portion of fresh haddock fillet

To fry white fish

1 portion fish (See under poaching.)
1 level tablespoon flour
pinch salt, shake pepper
50 g fat
sprig parsley
slice lemon ①

1. Wash the fish in cold water.
2. Pat dry on kitchen paper.
3. Put a plate or dish to warm and also crumpled tissue or kitchen paper on a tin or enamel plate to drain fish *after* frying.
4. Put flour, salt and pepper on to a plate or piece of greaseproof paper.
5. Press one side of the fish into the flour. Turn the fish and do the same on the second side, making sure that both sides are evenly coated. Then lift the fish on to a clean plate.
6. Heat the fat in the frying-pan; choose a small pan for one piece of fish. When the fat gives a faint haze, or a cube of bread turns golden brown in 1 minute, it is time to put in the fish.
7. Put the fish gently into the fat. (If you drop it in you will have fat splashing up.)
8. Cook fish for 2 minutes, then turn over. The easiest way to do this is to have a fish slice in one hand *and* a palette knife in the other. Slip the fish slice under the fish and hold the knife over the top of the fish to stop it breaking, and turn slowly.
9. Fry for 2 minutes on the second side; turn down heat.

Thin fillets fish (plaice—whiting) need another minute—total cooking time, 5 minutes.

Thick fillets fish (cod—haddock, etc.) need another 3–4 minutes—total cooking time, 7–8 minutes.

Whole fish or thick steaks of fish (cod, haddock) need another 4–5 minutes—total cooking time, 8–9 minutes.

Test before removing from fat to see if they are cooked.

10. Lift fish from pan on to paper, drain for 1 minute, then lift on to hot serving plate or dish.
11. Garnish with parsley and lemon.
12. (*a*) Your teacher may want you to strain left-over fat into a basin.
(*b*) Wipe the greasy frying-pan with kitchen paper before washing.

Cutlets of cod grilled with tomatoes

Many people like fried potatoes with fried fish, but when you begin cooking, it is not easy to fry two kinds of foods perfectly at the same time, so serve fried fish with boiled or mashed potatoes and a green vegetable or peas. The recipe for fried potatoes is on page 158.

To grill white fish

1 portion fish (See under poaching)
15–25 g margarine or butter
pinch salt, shake pepper
sprig parsley, slice lemon ①

1. Light or switch on the grill; put a plate or serving dish to warm.
2. Wash fish in cold water.
3. Pat dry on kitchen paper.
4. Melt margarine, butter or fat.
5. Brush the wire grid or metal rack of the grill pan to prevent fish sticking. Or, to make washing up easier, cut a piece of foil a little larger than the fish, brush with melted fat, and put on the grid or rack.
6. Place the fish on this, brush with melted margarine or fat, sprinkle lightly with salt and pepper. You can add a squeeze of lemon juice for extra flavour.
7. Put under the hot grill and leave for 2–3 minutes until brown.

Thin fillets of plaice or whiting do not need turning. Lower heat of the grill and cook for a further 2–3 minutes—total cooking time, approximately 5 minutes.

Whole fish, thicker pieces of fillets or steaks of fish must be turned. Remove the pan from under the grill and turn fish with a fish slice underneath and a palette knife on top to support it and prevent it from breaking. Brush the second side of fish with melted fat, season lightly and put the pan back under the hot grill. Brown on the second side for 2–3 minutes. Lower heat and cook for a further 3–4 minutes—total cooking time, 9–10 minutes.

8. Test before lifting on to warm dish.
9. Garnish with parsley and lemon.

Halved tomatoes could be cooked at the same time. (See picture, page 119.)

Serve mashed or boiled potatoes and green vegetables with grilled fish. A sauce is not necessary, although you can make white, parsley or cheese sauce if you wish.

A piece of grilled fish can be covered with a tablespoon of grated cheese for the last 1–2 minutes of cooking. This gives a golden crust, and very good flavour, as well as adding *extra* protein.

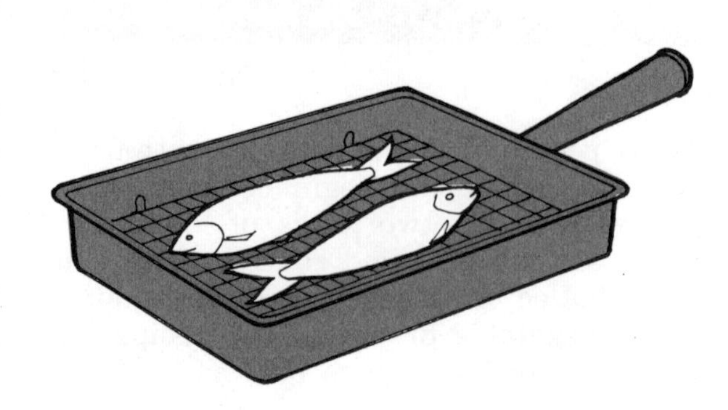

To bake white fish

1 portion fish
(See under poaching)
15–25 g margarine or butter
pinch salt, shake pepper
sprig parsley, slice lemon

1. Wash fish in cold water.
2. Pat dry on kitchen paper.
3. Grease a small casserole or dish.
4. Put in the fish—thin fillets may be folded to fit into the dish—add a light sprinkling of salt and a shake of pepper and a squeeze of lemon juice.
5. Spread the margarine over the fish.
6. Put a plate or serving dish to warm.
7. Cover the dish with a lid, greased foil or greaseproof paper.
8. Bake in the centre of a moderate oven (180–190°C—Gas Mark 4–5). Allow 12–15 minutes for thin fillets; 15–20 minutes for folded fillets, thick pieces of fillet; 20–25 minutes for whole fish or thick steaks of fish.
9. Lift from the dish on to the hot plate; garnish with parsley and lemon.

White fish (turbot) baked in the oven

Note: Fish may be wrapped in a parcel of greased foil and baked on a flat dish. This keeps in the flavour.
When fish is cooked in the oven, you can bake halved tomatoes in the same dish. Potatoes baked in their jackets could also be served, although these must be put into the oven *before* the fish. (See page 71.) Baked fish is more interesting with a stuffing. (See page 193.)

Steaming white fish

This method of cooking is generally used for fillets of plaice, sole, or whiting, or for the whole fish. It is considered the best way of cooking fish for an invalid or for young children.

To steam white fish

1 or 2 fillets plaice, sole, whiting; ② or whole fish
15 g butter or margarine
pinch salt, shake pepper
1 tablespoon milk
sprig parsley slice lemon

1. Cut away fins from the whole fish; wash the fish in cold water.
2. Pat dry on kitchen paper.
3. Choose an ovenproof plate large enough to fit safely over the top of a saucepan.
4. Half fill saucepan with water and carry it over to the cooker.
5. Grease the plate, add fish, folding the fillets if large; add salt, pepper and the rest of butter and milk.
6. Put the plate on top of the saucepan and cover with a second plate or with greased foil or greaseproof paper and the lid of the saucepan. Put serving plate or dish to warm.
7. Bring the water to the boil and lower heat so that it simmers steadily.
8. Allow 8–10 minutes for fillets of fish, or 12–15 minutes for whole fish.
9. Remove the top plate. Take the lower plate off the saucepan. Lift the fish on to the hot serving plate.
10. Garnish with a sprig of parsley and a slice of lemon.

Steamed fish can be served with a *white* or *parsley sauce*. The liquid on the plate can be strained into the sauce for extra flavour.

To cook oily fish

While most methods of cooking can be used for oily fish, these are the most suitable.

To poach oily fish

(used only for kippers.)

1 kipper or 2 kipper fillets
15 g margarine or butter
280 ml boiling water

1. Cut the fins off the sides of the kipper.
2. Wash kipper in cold water and pat it dry on kitchen paper.
3. Put the fish either into a large deep jug or lay it flat in a deep dish. Warm a plate or serving dish.
4. Pour the boiling water over the fish. Put a plate or paper on top of the container to keep in the steam.
5. Leave for 4 minutes. Lift the kipper from the water, hold it over the jug or dish for a short time to drain and put it on the plate.
6. Top with margarine.

This method gives a lightly cooked kipper which many people enjoy; it also prevents a strong smell of fish cooking. You can put the cooked kipper under the hot grill for 1 minute to crisp slightly.

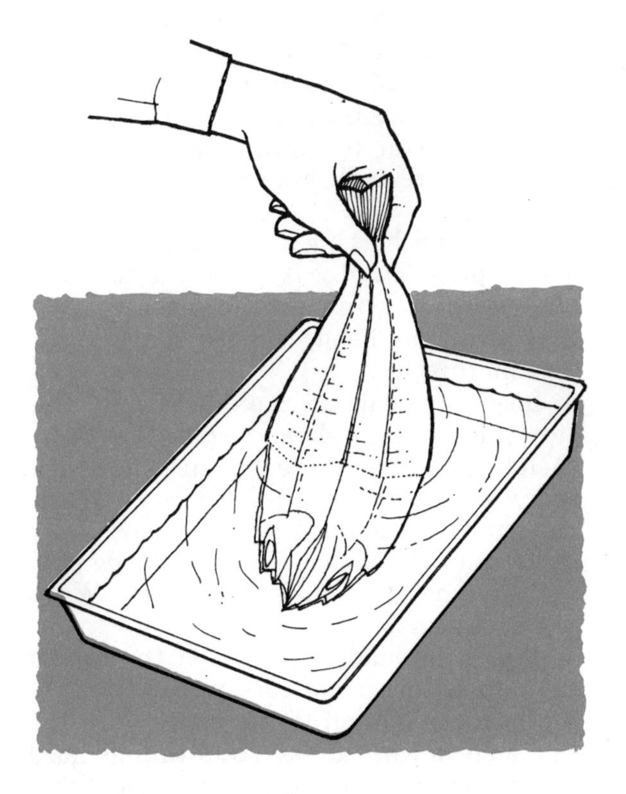

Taking bones out of herrings

Herrings contain many bones; the fishmonger will often take these out for you, but it is useful to know how it is done. These pictures will help you.

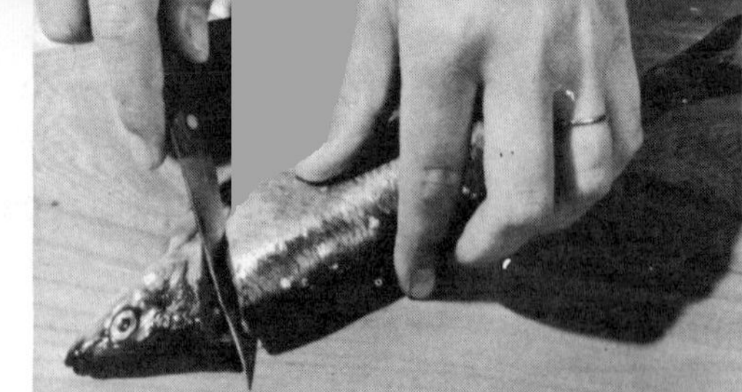

①

1. Wash the herring well. Put it on to a chopping board. It is useful to have newspaper to wrap up the pieces.
2. Cut off the head, using a sharp knife. (See picture 1.)
3. Insert the tip of the knife into the stomach of the fish and split the skin; then take out the inside. In large herrings there will be a soft or hard roe. Wash this, put it on a plate and throw away the rest of the inside. Next wash the fish, and then pat dry on kitchen paper. Wash your hands.
4. Rub a flat-bladed knife over the fish to take off loose scales. (See picture 2.)
5. Turn the fish on to the board with the cut side down. Press your thumb hard against the backbone. (See picture 3.)
6. When you turn the fish, you can take out the bones quite easily. (See picture 4.)
7. Put the roe back in the herring and cook by any method given.

②

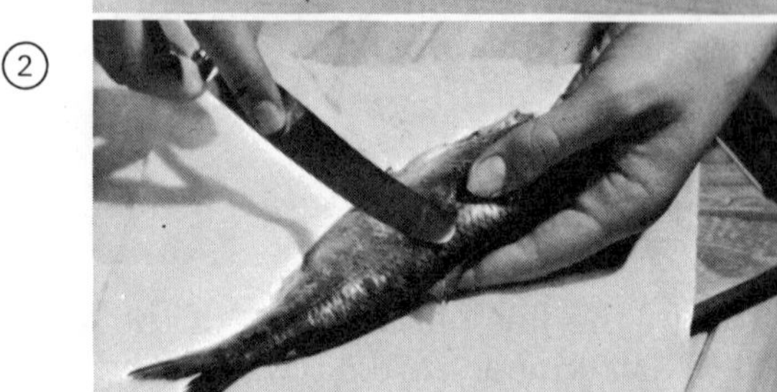

③

④

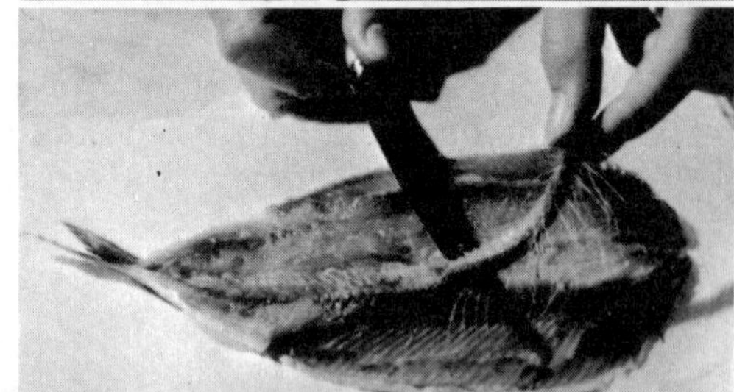

Fried oily fish

This method of cooking is used for all oily fish. Because of the natural oils in the fish, herrings, mackerel and sprats can be cooked in a dry frying-pan or with very little fat. A certain amount of oil is lost in smoking, so grease the pan for kippers and bloaters. Herrings, mackerel and bloaters are easier to cook and eat if the backbone has been removed. The pictures show how this is done. Cut the heads off sprats; cut the fins from kippers.

To fry oily fish

1 portion fish (This means whole herring, mackerel, bloater, kipper or about 6–8 sprats.)
good pinch salt (except with bloaters and kippers)
sprig parsley, slice lemon ①

1. Prepare fish as above, then wash and dry it on kitchen paper; sprinkle with a little salt and pepper.
2. You can cut 2 or 3 slits across the body of a whole fish. This helps it to cook more quickly. Put serving dish to warm.
3. Grease the pan only where necessary and warm it for 2 minutes over low heat.
4. Put the fish into the pan. Cook kippers and sprats for 2–3 minutes, herrings, mackerel and bloaters for 4 minutes. Turn and cook for the same time on the second side. Leave mackerel, which are large fish, for a further 2 minutes after turning.

Total cooking times:
kippers, sprats, 5–6 minutes
herrings, bloaters, 5–6 minutes
mackerel, 10 minutes

5. Test to see if the fish is cooked, then lift on to hot plate and garnish with parsley and lemon.

Fried herring in oatmeal

1. For 1 herring allow 1 level tablespoon medium or fine oatmeal, or rolled oats.
2. Put it on a plate or piece of greaseproof paper.
3. Add a good pinch of salt and a shake of pepper.
4. Coat the herring on both sides with oatmeal as you would coat fish in flour. (See page 118.)

5. Use 15 g (1 level tablespoon) only of fat, or use *no fat*. Sprinkle the bottom of the frying-pan with a very little salt.
6. Heat the fat or pan for 2–3 minutes. Put in herring and cook as before.

To grill oily fish

1 portion oily fish 
15 g margarine or fat

(Below) Grilling kippers. (Opposite) Grilled herrings

Herrings, mackerel, bloaters, kippers are suitable; sprats break easily when grilled.
1. Prepare, wash and dry the fish.
2. Grill as white fish. Total cooking time:
   4–5 minutes for kippers (these need not be turned)
   8 minutes for herrings and bloaters
   10 minutes for mackerel

To bake oily fish

1 portion oily fish	pinch salt
15 g margarine or fat	shake pepper
sprig parsley	(not with kippers or
slice lemon	bloaters) ①

Herrings, bloaters, mackerel, kippers and sprats are suitable.
1. Wash and dry the fish.
2. Cook as baked white fish in greased covered dish or foil. Allow:
   10 minutes for kippers and sprats. (See picture, page 129.)
   12–15 minutes for herrings (or 20 minutes when stuffed)
   20 minutes for mackerel

Oily fish is rarely *steamed*, although this could be done if you wish.

To cook smoked fish

The most usual way of cooking smoked fish such as haddock or cod is to poach it, either in water (see white fish, page 116) or half water and half milk.

To poach smoked fish

½ small smoked (Finnan) haddock or 100 g (1 portion) smoked haddock or cod fillet
280 ml milk and water *or* water
15 g margarine or butter ①

ɛeft) Poached portions of fresh haddock fillet ›pped with cheese sauce (pages 116 and 117)

The method of cooking is the same as for poached white fish. See page 116, but *do not* add salt as smoked haddock is salted. Allow approximately 5 minutes cooking time.

Serve with the piece of margarine or butter on top (see picture below).

Note: Another way to serve smoked haddock is with a poached egg. Lift the fish on to a hot serving plate or dish and put the egg on top.

What are their main nutrients?

white fish oily fish

Poached smoked haddock

16. MAKING JELLIES

THE easiest way to make a jelly is to use a flavoured packet.

Fruit jelly

1 packet fruit jelly hot water (see packet)	(4)

1. Dissolve the jelly as instructed on the packet; cool slightly.
2. Rinse out a basin or mould with *cold* water. This helps in turning out the jelly.

Fruit jelly

3. Pour the jelly into a mould and leave in a cool place to set. If putting into the refrigerator, make sure the liquid is no longer steaming.
4. *To turn out:*
(*a*) Put a serving plate or dish in clean cold water and shake it nearly dry. This will enable you to move the jelly into the right position on the dish without breaking it.
(*b*) Dip the mould into warm water for 5 seconds to loosen jelly.
(*c*) Put the plate over the top of the mould. Hold firmly and turn over so that the plate is now *under* the mould. Shake gently and lift away the mould.

Milk jelly

1 packet fruit jelly 140 ml hot water milk (approximately 420 ml)	(4)

1. Dissolve the jelly as instructed on the packet, but use only 140 ml of water.

Milk jelly

2. Allow to cool but *not* to set, then add enough cold milk to make up to the quantity of liquid given on the packet.
3. Pour the milk jelly into a mould. Leave to set and turn it out as in the picture.

Jelly with fruit

1 packet fruit jelly hot water (see packet) 1 banana 1 pear 1 tablespoon lemon juice	(4)

1. Measure out the water. Remove 2 tablespoons of this to make up for the lemon juice and juice in the fruit.
2. Make jelly, let it cool, add the prepared fruit, pour into mould and allow to set.
3. To keep the pear and banana a good colour, dip in lemon juice before putting into the jelly.

If you want to set fruit in layers in a jelly:

Arranging fruit in layers

(*a*) Pour some jelly into the mould and leave to set.
(*b*) Keep the rest of the jelly in a warm place so that it cools but does not set.
(*c*) Arrange fruit on the set jelly, cover with cold liquid jelly and leave to set again.
(*d*) Continue like this until all the fruit and jelly is used.

Any fresh fruits except pineapple can be added to a jelly. Canned fruit may be added. Use syrup as part of the liquid, and always use a little less than the amount of liquid given on the packet as canned fruit is moist.

Jelly with fruit

Fresh orange jelly

280 ml water	④
3 large oranges	
50 g sugar	
15 g powdered gelatine	
3 tablespoons water	

1. First grate the orange rind. To do this stand the grater on a plate, rub oranges against the fine side until all the orange-coloured peel has been removed. (You may hear this called the 'zest' of the orange.) Do not use the white pith, which is bitter and will spoil the taste of the jelly. (See picture, page 133.) Brush the grater hard with a pastry brush to take off the peel so that none is wasted.
2. Put the 280 ml water into a saucepan; add the grated orange rind and sugar.
3. Simmer for 10 minutes.
4. Put the gelatine and cold water into a basin, strain the very hot liquid over this and stir until the gelatine is dissolved.

Grating orange rind

5. Halve oranges, put over lemon squeezer, press hard and squeeze out all the juice. Add the juice to the gelatine liquid. Measure and add enough cold water to give a total of 560 ml.
6. Pour into a rinsed mould. Continue as for fruit jelly made from a packet.

What are their food values?

an ordinary jelly
milk jelly
fresh orange jelly

Taking juice from citrus fruit without a squeezer

The easiest and best way to remove juice from oranges and lemons is with a lemon squeezer. If you have no lemon squeezer, put the fruit for a minute in hot water to soften it. Cut in half and squeeze out the juice by hand, into a jug. (See picture.) Pour the juice through a strainer to remove any pips or tiny pieces of fruit pulp.

17. BAKED PUDDINGS

THESE puddings are easy to make and can be cooked when you are using the oven for meat or fish dishes.

Fruit charlotte

½ kg fruit	4 or 5 slices bread
75–100 g sugar	50–75 g margarine
(brown or white)	water ④

1. Grease an ovenproof dish.
2. Prepare and cook the fruit until soft, with *half* the sugar only, and the same amount of water as for fruit purée, (pages 104–105).
3. Cut the crusts off the bread—these can be dried and used for crumbs—page 179, and cut the bread into fingers.
4. Heat 50 g of the margarine in a frying-pan, cook half the fingers of bread on one side until golden; turn over and cook on the other side. Take out of the pan, put in the rest of the margarine, heat and fry a second batch of bread.
5. Put a layer of crisped bread at the bottom of an ovenproof dish and sprinkle with a little sugar.
6. Add *half* the fruit purée, then a layer of bread and a sprinkling of sugar.
7. Add the rest of the fruit and the last of the bread and sugar.
8. Bake in the centre of a very moderate oven (160°C—Gas Mark 3) for 40 minutes.

Another method

The picture on page 145 shows a rather special fruit charlotte. Use 6 or 7 slices of bread and 100 g margarine. Cut the bread into fingers and fry as in the recipe, but use the extra pieces of bread to go round the sides of a greased cake tin. Fill the tin as the recipe and cook as before, but you can turn the pudding out of the tin to serve it.

First ' rubbed in ' mixture

The top of fruit crumble is made by rubbing fat into flour in just the same way as for the beginning of many cakes—(see page 139) and pastry (see page 189).

Fruit crumble

200 g fruit ②
1–2 tablespoons water 25 g sugar

For the crumble:
50 g flour (plain or self-raising)
25 g margarine
25 g sugar

1. Put the prepared fruit into a small pie-dish—a 280 ml size.
2. Add the water. Use 2 tablespoons for hard fruit such as apples and plums, but 1 tablespoon for juicy fruits such as rhubarb and black currants. Put in the sugar.
3. Sieve flour into a mixing bowl; some people like to add a pinch of salt.
4. Add the margarine and rub in as described on page 139; add sugar.
5. Sprinkle the crumble mixture over the fruit; press down with the tips of your fingers; make sure no crumbs of flour, etc., are on the rim of the dish. (See picture.)
6. Bake in the centre of a moderate oven (180°C—Gas Mark 4) for hard fruits and allow 35 minutes; (190°C—Gas Mark 5) for soft fruits and allow 25 minutes.

While either of these puddings is cooking make custard sauce, (page 106), to serve with it.

What is the food value?

fruit charlotte
fruit crumble

18. MORE MENUS FOR DINNER

NOW you have learned about cooking fish, jellies and more puddings, there are many more meals you can make for dinner. Here are some ideas, but you will be able to work out others for yourself.

In the first dinner menus (page 112) and in the following menus, you will notice how the cooking is planned. If the main dish is a filling one, then the pudding is light. The oven is not put on just for one dish; it is used for 2 dishes or for most of the meal.

Grilled fish, tomatoes, mashed potatoes, peas; jelly and cream or creamy packet topping

Fried pork chops, apple sauce, potatoes, cauliflower; rice cream

Baked fish, jacket potatoes, carrots; bread and butter pudding

Grilled bacon and sausages, grilled tomatoes, and/or a green vegetable such as spinach; stewed dried fruit and custard

Poached white fish, white or cheese sauce, mashed potatoes, carrots; jelly and blancmange or steamed pudding.

Fried herrings in oatmeal, cauliflower, peas; ice-cream and chocolate sauce

Roast lamb, mint sauce, gravy, boiled potatoes, peas; fruit crumble

(Put the crumble in the coolest part of the oven.)

Hot steamed canned pudding may be served topped with ice-cream for a change

19. 'RUBBED IN' METHOD OF MIXING

THIS way of mixing is suitable for the crumble topping in fruit crumble and for many biscuits and cakes. These are some of the important things to remember:

1. Weigh the ingredients carefully.
2. Wash then dry your hands carefully.
3. Rub fat into the flour with gentle movements. If you are too rough and press the fat into the flour very hard, the mixture becomes too sticky to handle. Use the forefinger and thumb of each hand, or the tips of your fingers, *not* the palm of your hand. (See picture.)
4. When you add liquid, do this slowly. If you put in too much you *spoil* biscuits or cakes.
5. Make sure the oven is the right temperature for baking.
6. Where dried fruit is used this must be clean. Wash and dry it well or rub in flour on a clean tea towel.
7. When making cakes, grease tin or tins with melted fat and a pastry brush, or a very small amount of fat on a piece of clean greaseproof paper.

Biscuits and cakes

The numbers indicate *how many* biscuits or cakes are made.

Vanilla biscuits

100 g flour (either self-raising or plain flour with 1 level teaspoon baking powder)
50 g margarine
50 g sugar
few drops vanilla essence
1–2 *teaspoons* milk
To sprinkle over biscuits
1 teaspoon sugar ⑩-⑪

1. Sieve the flour, or flour and baking powder, into a mixing bowl. Some people like to add a pinch of salt.
2. Rub in the margarine with the forefinger and thumb of each hand until it is like crumbs; or use your finger tips.
3. Add the sugar.
4. Mix the vanilla essence with 1 teaspoon milk and add to the biscuit mixture.

5. Knead (see page 42) very hard. This is the difference between making biscuits and pastry. You can be firm with biscuit mixture but must be gentle with pastry mixture.
6. The mixture should form one ball. If too dry, add another teaspoon of milk. This should be enough.
7. Put on to the pastry board and divide into about 10 or 11 equal-sized pieces.
8. Roll each piece into a neat ball.
9. Place on 2 ungreased baking trays with plenty of room for them to spread out.
10. Flatten slightly with the back of a fork or your hand (see picture, this page).
11. Bake in the centre of a moderate oven (180–190°C—Gas Mark 4–5) for about 15 minutes until golden.
12. Lift out of the oven, cool for 5 minutes *on tins* so that the biscuits do not break, then lift with a palette knife and place on a wire cooling tray (see opposite).
13. When quite cold, store in an airtight tin *away* from bread, pastry or cakes.

This recipe can be varied
1. Replace 1 level tablespoon flour with 1 level tablespoon cocoa for chocolate biscuits. Grease tin before baking.
2. Omit vanilla essence; add 1 teaspoon finely grated lemon or orange rind to the flour and mix with lemon or orange juice, instead of water.
3. Add 25 g chopped glacé cherries with the sugar; grease tin before baking.

SCUITS

Cake mixture by rubbing in method

Used for: large cake, rock buns, jam buns, lemon buns

Rock buns

⑤-⑥

100 g flour (self-raising, or plain flour with 1 level teaspoon baking powder)
50 g margarine, 50 g sugar
1 *small* egg (see point 3)
50 g dried fruit (all currants, or 25 g currants, 25 g sultanas)

1. Grease a flat baking tin. Sieve flour or flour and baking powder. Some people like to add a pinch of salt.
2. Rub in margarine, add the sugar and dried fruit.
3. Break the egg into a small basin, then add to the flour mixture—this means the flour with the ingredients added at stage 2. Your teacher may tell you to beat it with a fork then add it to the flour, *or* she may prefer you to use ½ beaten egg only and someone else to use the other ½ egg.
4. The mixture should 'stand up' in points when you mix it with a palette

knife. If it is too stiff, add a few drops of milk.

5. Put 5–6 equal-sized 'heaps' on to the baking tin, allowing space for them to spread. Use 2 teaspoons or a spoon and knife to do this. (See picture, page 142.)

6. Sprinkle lightly with sugar before cooking, to give the buns a better look.

7. Bake towards the top (or top and bottom in most electric ovens) of a moderately hot oven (200–220°C—Gas Mark 6–7) for 12–15 minutes.

8. Lift very carefully with a palette knife on to a wire cooling tray. (See picture on right.)

Lemon buns

Follow the recipe for rock buns, but use the grated rind of 1 lemon to flavour.

Jam buns

Use the same mixture as for rock buns, but no dried fruit. Instead, you will need 1 tablespoon jam to put on the buns.

1. Either make the buns as for rock buns or, for a neater jam bun, omit any milk and roll the mixture into balls. Put on to a baking tin, as shown overleaf.

2. Put a teaspoon of flour on a plate.
3. Dip your finger in this, then press into the centre of each bun to make a hollow.
4. Put a little jam into this, using two teaspoons, then pull the edges of the cake mixture over the jam.
5. Sprinkle with sugar if desired, and bake as before.

(Above) Rock buns and jam buns (pages 142–3)
(Colour) Fruit charlotte with bread fingers (page 135)

SUGAR

Fruit cake

Use double the amount of ingredients as for rock buns. You may use only 1 egg to 200 g flour.

1. Grease a 15 cm round cake tin or ½ kg loaf tin. Shake in a little flour and turn the tin round until covered *very lightly*.
2. Make the mixture as for rock buns, but mix with a wooden spoon. Add enough milk for the mixture to drop from the spoon when shaken *firmly*.
3. Put into a tin and bake in the centre of a moderate oven (180–190°C—Gas Mark 4–5), for approximately 1 hour.
4. *Test* the cake to see if it is cooked. It should have shrunk away from the sides of the tin. When pressed on top, it should feel quite firm.
5. Turn the cake very carefully out of the tin and put on to a wire cooling tray.

This recipe can be varied for large cakes

1. Sieve ½–1 teaspoon mixed spice with flour.
2. Add finely grated rind 1 orange or 1 lemon to flour, and mix with orange or lemon juice in place of milk.
3. Add chopped dates instead of currants and sultanas.

'his page) Fruit cake
.eft) Ice-cream and chocolate sauce (page 81)

20. MEALS WITH CHEESE

ON pages 47–48, cheese is used as the main ingredient in a salad for a light meal. A cheese sauce (page 70) adds protein to a meal of mixed vegetables. If you have bread and butter, cheese and fruit, you have a simple but very nourishing meal. There are many cooked dishes in which cheese is one of the main ingredients; because it is a fine body-building food, you can serve these for dinner in place of meat or fish.

When you cook with cheese

Buy the right kind of cheese; not every cheese is suitable for use in cooking. The most popular kind for cooking as well as for eating uncooked is Cheddar, but Lancashire or Cheshire cheese give a good flavour. Do not overcook any dish containing cheese; try to serve the dish just after it is cooked, as cheese dishes spoil if they are kept waiting.

Macaroni cheese

②

40–50 g macaroni (50 g gives a more solid dish)
½ level teaspoon salt
280 ml cheese sauce (page 70 or 152)
For the topping
1 tablespoon grated cheese
1 tablespoon breadcrumbs
To garnish
parsley, tomato

1. Bring 1 litre water to the boil.
2. Add the salt and put in the macaroni. You may need to break this into convenient sized pieces.
3. When the water returns to the boil, lower the heat and cook until the macaroni is tender but *not* too soft. Quick cooking

Macaroni cheese

thin macaroni takes approximately 7 minutes boiling; the thicker kind needs 20 minutes. To test if cooked, press one piece of macaroni against the side of the saucepan with a fork; it will break when cooked.

4. While the macaroni is cooking, prepare the sauce and the topping.
5. Stand a strainer or sieve in a mixing bowl and strain the macaroni. If you wish, you can use some of the macaroni liquid in the cheese sauce instead of all milk.
6. Tip the macaroni into the sauce, mix well, then put into a pie-dish.
7. Sprinkle grated cheese and breadcrumbs over the top of the mixture.
8. Either put under the grill for 3–5 minutes to brown, or towards the top of a moderately hot oven (200°C—Gas Mark 6) for 15 minutes.
9. Garnish with small pieces of parsley or with a sliced tomato.

Put the saucepan to soak in cold water

To serve with macaroni cheese:

As macaroni is a filling food, you will not need potatoes; a green vegetable or a mixed salad is the best.

Cauliflower cheese with tomatoes

Cauliflower cheese

1 small cauliflower
280 ml cheese sauce (page 70 or 152)
For the topping
1 tablespoon grated cheese
1 tablespoon breadcrumbs
To garnish
1 teaspoon chopped parsley

Instead of serving cooked cauliflower with a cheese sauce (page 152), you can turn it into a more attractive looking dish in this way.

1. Prepare the cauliflower (leave whole). Choose an ovenproof serving dish that just fits the cauliflower and allows it to stand upright when cooked. It must also take the sauce.
2. Cook cauliflower in boiling salted water until tender.
3. While it is cooking, prepare the cheese sauce and topping; warm the dish.
4. Strain the cauliflower, stand the colander in a mixing bowl so that you keep the water; some of this can be used in the sauce instead of all milk.
5. Put the cauliflower into the serving

dish, *switch on or light the grill.* If you cook and serve this dish quickly, you keep more of the important vitamin C that is in cauliflower.
6. Pour the cheese sauce carefully over the top of the cauliflower.
7. Sprinkle on the cheese and crumbs; brown for about 3 minutes under the grill.
8. Add chopped parsley and serve at once.

To serve with cauliflower cheese
Mashed or boiled potatoes or carrots are a good vegetable to serve with this. Or you could toast slices of bread under the grill before browning the cauliflower cheese.
The toast can either be served separately or cut into triangles and arranged round the dish.
Grilled tomatoes also go well with cauliflower.

Cheese bread and butter pudding
This is another easy and very delicious cheese dish. (See picture, page 164.)
Follow the directions for bread and butter pudding on page 78.
Instead of adding dried fruit to the bread and butter, add 50 g grated cheese.
Instead of adding sugar to the egg, add $\frac{1}{2}$ level teaspoon salt, a shake of pepper and $\frac{1}{2}$ teaspoon made mustard.
Serve with a salad, raw or cooked tomatoes.

White sauce—'roux' method
On pages 69–70, one way of making white sauce and other similar sauces was given. Many people feel that the following way of making a sauce, by the 'roux' method, is better. It is not quite so easy as the blended method, for you must be very careful about *how* you add the milk to the 'roux'.

25 g margarine	pinch salt
25 g flour	shake pepper
280 ml milk	

1. Heat the margarine in a small saucepan.
2. When this has melted, take the saucepan off the heat and add the flour.
3. Stir this into the margarine with a wooden spoon until well mixed.

4. Lower the heat, then put the saucepan back on the gas ring or boiling plate and cook for 2–3 minutes, stirring well. During this time you will find the margarine and flour mixture, called the 'roux', begins to look dry and crumbly. It should *not* change colour. If it does begin to go a golden colour, the heat is too high, so take the pan off at once.
5. Take the pan off the heat when the 'roux' is dry. *Gradually* stir in the milk (or you may be using vegetable stock or macaroni stock *and* milk, so mix these together to give 280 ml). Add the liquid *slowly*, stirring well, so that the sauce keeps smooth, all the time.
6. Add salt and pepper.
7. Put the sauce back over the heat and bring to the boil, stirring all the time.
8. Lower the heat and continue cooking the sauce for 3 minutes, stirring all the time (page 70). Point 5 tells you about stirring a sauce. Taste the sauce and, if necessary, add a little more salt and pepper.
9. If you wish to keep the sauce hot without a skin forming, cover with a round of damp greaseproof paper.

How to vary white sauce

Hard-boiled egg sauce

1. Hard boil 1 or 2 eggs. (See page 46.)
2. Remove the shells; chop the eggs.
3. Make the white sauce and, when this is cooked, add the eggs.

Cheese sauce

1. Grate 50–100 g Cheddar cheese finely.
2. Make the white sauce, adding a pinch of dried mustard to the flour.
3. When the sauce is cooked, stir in the cheese.
4. Cook for 1 minute only over a low heat until the cheese has melted.

Parsley sauce

1. Chop enough washed and dried parsley to give 2–3 teaspoons.
2. Make the white sauce and, when this is cooked, add the finely chopped parsley.

What are their main food values?

macaroni cheese
cauliflower cheese
cheese bread and butter pudding

21. TOASTED AND FRIED SNACKS

THERE are many times when we do not need a substantial meal, but just a light and satisfying snack.
Choose protein foods where possible, and serve hot snacks as soon as they are made so that they do not spoil.

Cheese on toast

1 slice bread ①
little butter or margarine
1 slice Cheddar or processed cheese

1. Heat the grill. Put a plate to warm.
2. Toast the bread on both sides and spread with butter on one side.
3. Cover the buttered side with cheese, and put back under the hot grill until the cheese begins to melt and bubble. It may just turn golden brown. This takes about 3 minutes.
4. Do not overcook, otherwise the cheese becomes tough. After toasting, the crusts can be cut from the bread, but if left, you have a more substantial meal.

Ways to vary cheese on toast

You can serve *toasted cheese* by itself, or with a green salad. You can make it more interesting if you add:

Tomatoes
Use either sliced, raw tomatoes, or grill halved tomatoes at the same time as the cheese. If you like, put a slice of tomato on top of the cheese before grilling it. (See pictures, pages 153 and 155.)

Bacon
Remove the rind from 1 or 2 rashers. Put the bacon under the grill at the same time as the cheese. Arrange on top of the toasted cheese when cooked. (See opposite.)

Prunes
Drain 2 or 3 cooked prunes from juice, put under grill at the same time as the cheese. Arrange on top of the toasted cheese when cooked. (See opposite.)

Pineapple rings
Drain 1 or 2 rings of canned pineapple from syrup. Put under the grill at the same time as the cheese. When cooked, arrange on top. (See opposite.)

Sardines
Put 1 or 2 sardines on the cheese before it goes under the grill, *or* melt cheese first, add sardine and warm for 1 minute. (See opposite.)

Grilled mushrooms
Wash 2 or 3 small mushrooms well. Your teacher will tell you if you should skin them. Some very good mushrooms do not need skinning and keep more of their flavour. Keep whole or slice thickly. Heat 15 g margarine or fat in the grill pan; add the mushrooms. Put the rack on the grill pan and make the toast, etc. By the time the cheese has melted, the mushrooms will be cooked. (See opposite.)

Sardines on toast

①

1 slice bread
little margarine or butter
2–3 sardines
sprig parsley

1. Heat grill and put a plate to warm.
2. Toast bread on both sides; butter on one side.
3. Either put sardines whole on toast, *or* mash them in a basin first.

4. Put the toast back under a hot grill for 2 minutes.
5. Arrange parsley on top.

To serve with sardines

Hard-boiled egg
Hard boil an egg (page 46), shell, slice and arrange it on top of sardines after they have been heated under the grill.

Tomatoes
Slice a tomato, arrange on the buttered toast, then add sardines.

Cheese
Put whole or mashed sardines on the toast, top with grated cheese and heat for 2 minutes under the grill.

Beans on toast

1 small can or portion beans in tomato sauce ①
1 slice bread
little butter or margarine

1. Heat grill and put a plate to warm.
2. Heat beans as directed on the can. Do not overcook, as the beans will break and become too salt.
3. Toast bread on both sides; spread with butter on one side.
4. Put toast on the plate and pile the hot beans on top.

Put the saucepan to soak in cold water.

To serve with beans on toast

Grilled bacon
Remove rinds from rashers of bacon and put beside the bread on grid of the grill pan, *or* make the toast, spread with butter, put on a plate and keep warm. Then grill the bacon.

Cheese
Toast cheese as on page 153, and top with the beans *or* sprinkle grated cheese over the beans.

Grilled tomatoes
Halve or slice tomatoes, and grill at the same time as you toast the bread.
Do not overcook the tomatoes as they lose flavour.

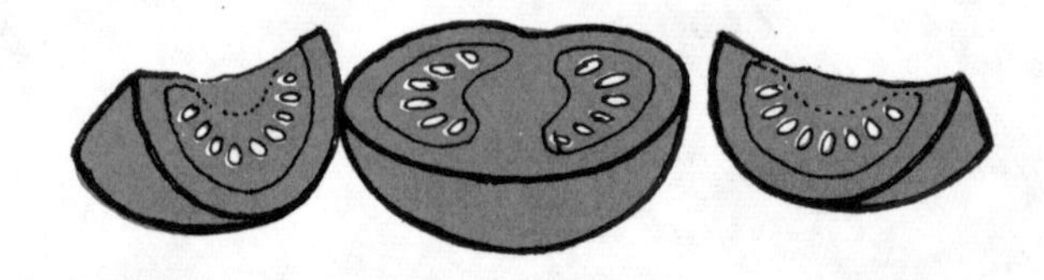

Spaghetti on toast

small can or portion of spaghetti 
with tomato and cheese sauce
1 slice bread
little butter or margarine

1. Heat grill. Put plate to warm.
2. Heat spaghetti as directed on the can.
3. Toast bread on both sides. Spread with butter on one side.
4. Top with hot spaghetti.

Put the saucepan to soak in cold water.

To serve with spaghetti on toast

Bacon
Remove rinds from rashers of bacon and put beside bread on the grid of the grill pan, *or* make the toast, spread with butter, put on a plate and keep warm. Then grill the bacon.

Poached or fried egg
See pages 52-3 and 58-59.

Cheese
Cover toast with a slice of cheese, melt under grill and top with hot spaghetti. Do not overcook the cheese, as it will become tough and may burn.

Poached egg on heated beans in tomato sauce, served on toast (see page 59)

Fried snacks

There are a number of fried foods that can be served as a quick snack. Many of them have been described already:

fried eggs
fried sausages
bacon and egg
bacon and tomato (pages 52-54)

You can make these more satisfying if you add beans or spaghetti, or serve them with fried potatoes.

Fried potatoes

These may be cooked in two ways—in a pan of deep fat (which you will be learning about later) *or* in less fat in an ordinary frying-pan. This is generally known as shallow frying. You have already used this method of cooking when you fried meat and fish. It is not difficult providing you remember these important points about frying.

First, safety

1. When using fat, be extra careful about turning frying-pan handles *away* from the edge of the cooker, for even a splash of hot fat can burn badly.
2. Never carry pans containing hot fat about in the kitchen. When you have finished using the pan, leave it on the cooker for a short time to allow the fat to cool slightly.
3. If a little fat splashes on the floor, wipe it up at once.

Good frying of potatoes

1. Your teacher will tell you which fat she wishes you to use.
2. Make sure the fat is the right heat *before* you start to cook the potatoes.
3. *Dry* the potatoes very thoroughly before frying.
4. Watch the heat as the potatoes fry, *turn down* after they go into the fat so that they brown steadily and are cooked through to the middle.

To fry potatoes

1 large potato ①
50 g fat

1. Peel the potato; wash it in cold water and dry
2. You can fry sliced potatoes. For these, you cut the potato in slices about 3–4 mm thick. For chipped potatoes, cut thicker slices about 6–8 mm thick and divide these

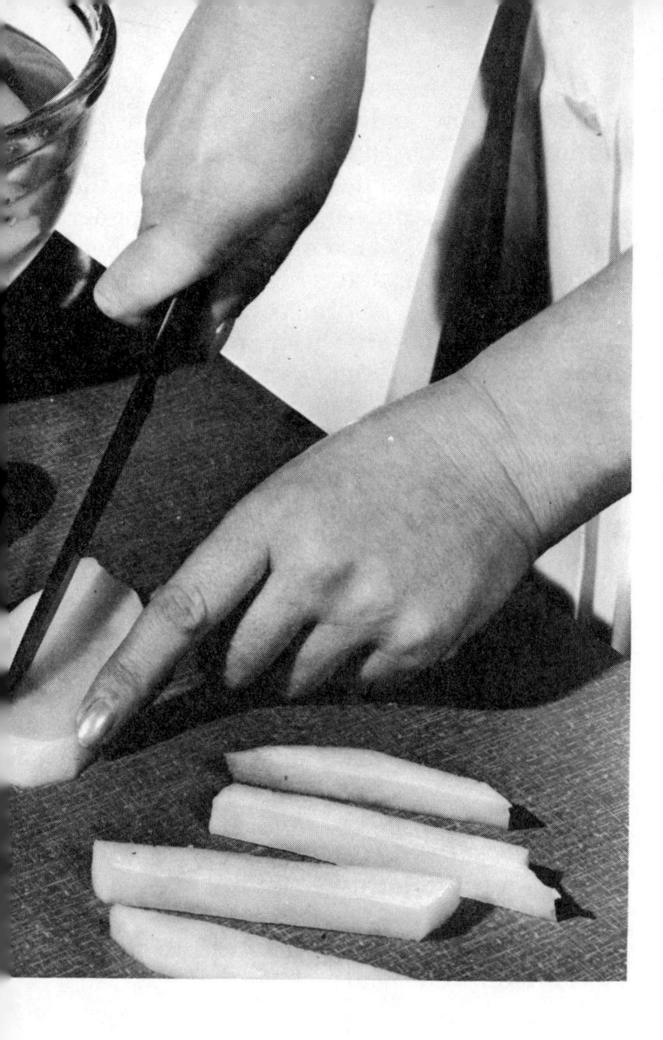

into fingers about 6–8 mm wide. (See picture on left.)

3. Put into a dry tea towel or kitchen paper and leave until ready to fry. (See picture, page 160.)

4. Arrange crumpled tissue or kitchen paper on a tin for draining; put a plate or serving dish to warm.

5. Heat the fat; test to see if ready with a small piece of bread. This should go golden brown in 1 minute. If you test with a piece of potato instead, the fat should bubble hard round this. If using cooking fat, you will see a faint haze. If your teacher wishes you to use oil instead of fat, she will tell you about heating and testing this.

6. Take potatoes over to the cooker *before* the fat is hot. Also take the piece of bread for testing, a fish slice, and the tin with draining paper. If you do this, you cannot forget the fat and it will not become overheated.

7. When the fat is ready, put in just enough potatoes to cover the bottom of the pan. If any are left, keep these covered with a cloth or paper so that they do not lose colour.

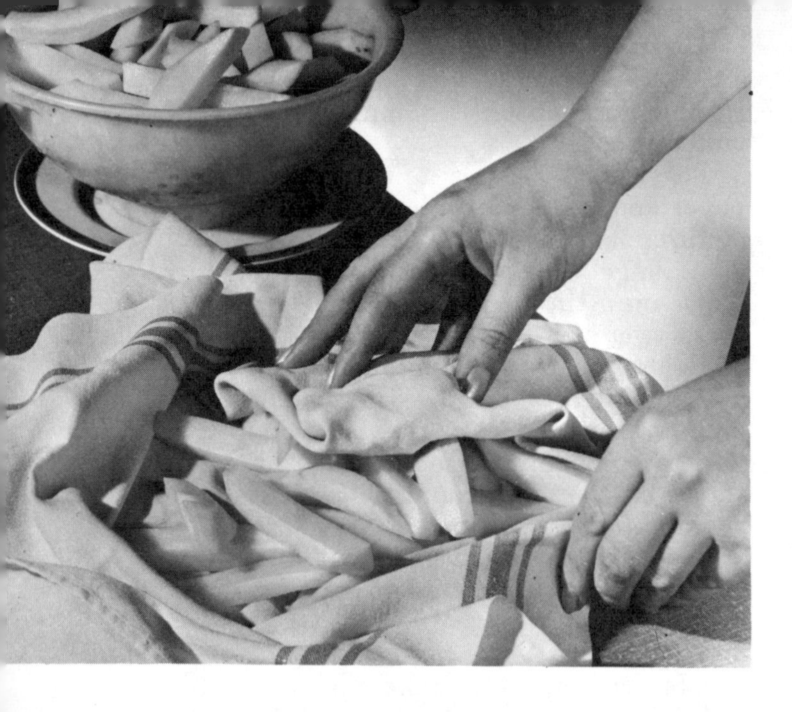

8. When the potatoes are put into the hot fat, lower the heat so that they cook steadily, but *not too quickly*. Fry for 2 minutes, when they should be golden brown on the under side. Turn over with the fish slice and cook on the second side for the same time. Thin slices may now be ready, but for thicker chips turn the heat very low and leave for another 1–2 minutes to cook through.

9. Lift potatoes out of the pan with the fish slice; put on to the draining paper for 1 minute. You can then put them into the serving dish.

10. If you have more potatoes to fry, reheat the fat before these are put in, and cook as before. Keep the first lot of fried potatoes hot while you cook the second.

11. Allow the fat in the pan to cool slightly, then pour or strain it into a basin to use again.

Wipe the frying-pan out with paper before washing up.

Fats to use for frying potatoes

Cooking fat, bought in packets
Lard, bought in packets
Well clarified dripping, which must be well cleaned for frying (pages 96-97)
Oil, which you buy in bottles

What are their food values?

cheese on toast, sardines on toast, beans on toast

What can you serve with these to make a well-balanced meal?

22. A GOOD TEA

If you have supper or dinner in the evening, tea-time will be a light meal. You can serve:

tiny sandwiches, bread and butter, or scones and butter, jam or honey, biscuits, cake and tea

Many people prefer to have a more filling tea and then just a milk drink in the evening. This is better for children who are going to bed early. If tea is to be the last meal of the day, serve protein foods as well as bread and butter, cake and tea. Often this is called 'high tea'. Many supper menus could be served for high tea. Pudding can replace cake.

Here are more ideas for you:
Sandwiches, fruit salad, biscuits, tea
Cheese on toast, salad, cake, tea
Sardines on toast, raw tomatoes, biscuits, fresh fruit, tea
Macaroni cheese, lettuce, tomato, fruit jelly, tea
Baked beans in tomato sauce served on toast with egg *or* bacon and tomato, (See pictures, pages 157 and 163) fresh orange jelly
Cold ham and salad, fried potatoes, ice-cream and fruit, tea

You may prefer a milky drink instead of tea.

This picture shows a new way to serve cheese on toast—topped with a ring of raw apple. Do this just before serving, so

that the apple keeps white. In the centre there is an olive; you could add a halved walnut instead.

Setting the tea table

If you are having a light tea, for each person you need:

cup, saucer, teaspoon, small plate, tea knife and napkin

You also need:

teapot, hot water jug, milk jug, sugar bowl, an extra bowl into which cold tea from the cups can be poured

plates for cake, bread and butter, jam dish and spoon

a knife to cut a large cake

For a high tea you will need to add:

knives, forks, dessertspoons and forks, serving dishes (depending on the food) and heatproof mats

A light tea can be served on a small table; there is no need to sit round a table.

Put a pretty traycloth on a tray. Set cups, saucers, spoons, teapot, etc., on this. If possible, each person has a small table with their plate, knife and napkin, and when the tea is poured out, the cups are brought round.

If you set tea on a table, the teapot, etc., and all the cups are put on the right hand of whoever is pouring out. Make sure the handles of the teapot and water jug are *not* sticking out over the edge of the table—otherwise people moving about may knock them over.

Use a gay tablecloth for tea and small napkins. Many people today use paper ones to save washing. Choose these to match the cloth and fold neatly.

Flowers on the table. At any meal, a small bowl of flowers makes the table look attractive. Do not use high vases that could be knocked over. See sketch.

(Right) Baked beans in tomato sauce with bacon and tomato (a good meal for high tea) (page 156)

23. STEWS AND CASSEROLES OF MEAT

CHEAPER meats give delicious meals in a stew or cooked in a casserole in the oven, as the long, slow cooking time makes the meat very tender.

These are the most usual cuts of meat for easy stews:

Beef

chuck or flank. (You can ask for stewing steak, which is generally sold in one or two large thick slices.)

Mutton or *lamb*

middle or scrag end of neck (sold cut in pieces).

Pork and *Veal*

these are rarely used in simple stews.

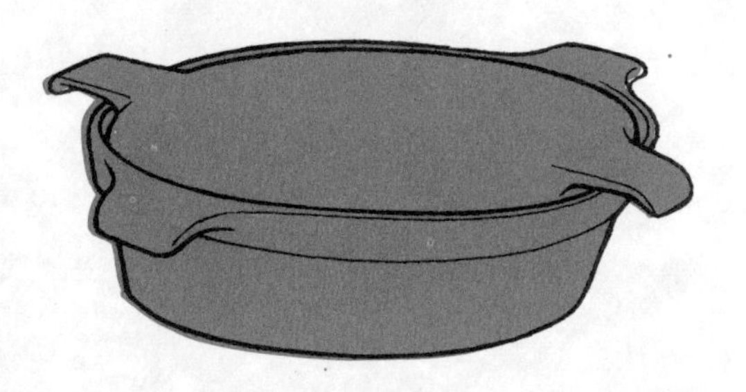

Beef and vegetable stew

200 g stewing steak ②-③
1 large carrot
1 onion
small piece of turnip or stick celery
15 g (1 level tablespoon) fat
420 ml brown stock
½ level teaspoon salt
shake pepper
1 level tablespoon flour

To garnish
2 teaspoons chopped parsley

The stock is made by simmering bones, or with water and a stock cube or gravy browning. (See page 90.)

1. Wash the meat, pat dry on kitchen paper and put on a chopping board.
2. Cut into 2½ cm squares; take away any gristle.
3. Peel the vegetables and cut into neat pieces.

Left) Cheese bread and butter pudding (page 151)

4. Melt the fat in the bottom of the saucepan. Choose one with a well fitting lid.
5. Put the meat and vegetables into the saucepan. Fry in the fat for 1 minute. Turn over and fry for the same time on the other side.
6. Add all the stock except for 4 tablespoons, the ½ teaspoon salt, and pepper.
7. Bring the liquid to simmering point, put a lid on the pan and simmer for 2 hours.
8. Look once or twice to see that the stew is not cooking too quickly; if it is, lower the heat.
9. Put the flour into a basin and blend with the 4 tablespoons of stock. Take this over to the saucepan, pour into the stew and stir with a wooden spoon to prevent the mixture becoming lumpy.
10. Cook for another 15 minutes, stirring from time to time. Add a little more salt and pepper if needed.
11. While the stew is cooking, put a serving dish to warm.
12. Spoon the stew into the dish and garnish with chopped parsley.

Serve the stew with a green vegetable and boiled or mashed potatoes, and mustard.

How to vary stews

1. Add peas during cooking; put in a good pinch of dried herbs.
2. Open a small can of baked beans in tomato sauce; add towards the end of the cooking time.
3. Choose several kinds of vegetables and add to the stew after 1 hour's cooking so that they remain a good colour. (See pictures below and on page 167.)

Beef and vegetable casserole

You need exactly the same ingredients, but use *just* 300 ml brown stock as the liquid does not evaporate in a casserole as it does in a saucepan.

1. Cut the meat as before.
2. Put the flour on a plate or piece of greaseproof paper, roll each piece of meat in the flour until well covered. Use *all* the flour. (For extra flavour, blend ½ level teaspoon mustard with the flour.)
3. Heat the fat in a saucepan, fry the meat and vegetables for 2 minutes, then lift these into an ovenproof casserole.
4. Add salt and pepper to the stock; pour over the meat and vegetables.
5. Put a lid or piece of foil over the casserole.
6. Cook for 2 hours in the middle of a very moderate oven (150–170°C—Gas Mark 2–3).

Serve with a green vegetable and boiled or jacket potatoes. Large potatoes will need 2 hours at this oven temperature.

Note: You could cook a rice pudding in the coolest part of the oven at the same time as the casserole.

Mutton or lamb stew or casserole

Follow the directions for a beef stew or casserole, but use 300 g scrag or middle neck of mutton or lamb instead of 200 g stewing beef. You need more mutton than beef because of the weight of the bones. If the mutton is very fat, cut the fat away before cooking otherwise the stew will be greasy. (See picture above.) One of the best ways of using mutton or lamb is in a hotpot. A recipe is given on the next page.

Hotpot

Hotpot

$\frac{3}{4}$ kg potatoes ④
2 large onions
$\frac{1}{2}$ kg middle neck of mutton
$\frac{1}{2}$ level teaspoon salt
shake pepper
280 ml stock (See page 90.)
25 g margarine

1. Peel potatoes and cut into slices 6–8 mm thick. Put in a basin of clean water until ready to use so that they keep white.
2. Peel the onions; cut into thin slices.
3. Wash the meat; pat dry in kitchen paper. If the meat is very fat, cut this away.
4. Stir the salt and pepper into the stock, to make sure it is evenly seasoned.
5. Lift potatoes out of the water and dry on a cloth.
6. Use half the margarine to grease a casserole.
7. Arrange one-third of the potatoes at the bottom of the casserole; add half the onions and half the meat.
8. Arrange more potatoes over this layer; add the rest of the onions and meat.

9. Cover with a final layer of potatoes, arranging them neatly as shown in picture.
10. Slowly pour on the seasoned stock and cover the potatoes with tiny pieces of margarine, then a piece of foil or the casserole lid.
11. Bake for 2 hours in the centre of a slow oven (150°C–Gas Mark 2).
12. Take the lid or foil off the casserole and cook for another 30 minutes so that the potatoes brown. (See picture, page 168.)

If more convenient, cook for 1½ hours in the centre of a very moderate oven (160°C—Gas Mark 3).

Serve a hotpot with a green vegetable.

The pictures of casseroles using meat and vegetables show the dishes *very* full, so that you can see the contents clearly. When you are preparing a casserole, choose a suitable size and do not fill it to overflowing.

What are its main food values?

Meat cooked in a stew or casserole with vegetables.

24. USING MINCED BEEF

MINCED beef is an economical way of using meat. Because raw minced beef spoils easily, store with care in a cool larder or refrigerator.
Minced beef makes a good stew; there are two ways of making this. The first method given on this page makes the meat more moist and tender; the second method is a little easier.

Mince

Both recipes need:

25 g fat (4)
1 medium-sized onion
15 g flour
280 ml stock
200 g minced beef
$\frac{1}{4}$ level teaspoon salt
shake pepper
To garnish: parsley, tomato

(The stock is made by simmering bones in water or with water and a stock cube or gravy browning.)

Method 1
After frying an onion in the fat, make a sauce by the 'blending' method (page 69). Then put the meat into this and cook it slowly, stirring the meat to stop it forming into lumps.

Method 2
The second way is to fry the meat first, then to add the ingredients for the sauce.

Method 1
1. Peel and chop the onion into small pieces.
2. Heat the fat in a saucepan and fry the onion for 2 minutes.
3. Put the flour into a basin and gradually add the stock, stirring well to blend smoothly.
4. Pour this into the saucepan, bring to the boil and cook for 3 minutes, stirring all the time.
5. Add the meat, salt and pepper. Put a tightly fitting lid on the saucepan.
6. Simmer for 1 hour; for the first 10–15

minutes keep breaking the meat into small pieces.

7. Put a rather deep serving dish to warm while the mince is cooking.

8. Taste meat before serving, adding extra salt and pepper if necessary.

9. Spoon the mince into the hot serving dish; garnish with parsley or sliced tomato.

Serve with boiled potatoes and a green vegetable for dinner, or with crisp toast for supper.

Method 2

1. Heat the fat and fry the onion as in Method 1.

2. Add the minced meat and fry this for 2 minutes, stirring well.

3. Continue as the recipe given in Method 1.

How to vary this stew

1. Fry skinned sliced tomato with the onion.

2. Add a good pinch of mixed herbs.

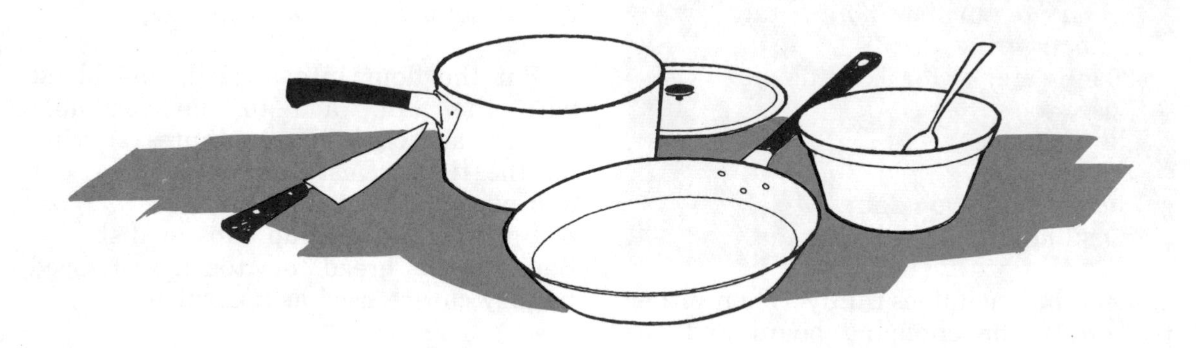

25. SOUPS

A VEGETABLE soup is easy to make and is a very good first course for dinner. You can make it into a light supper dish if you sprinkle grated cheese on top before serving.

Vegetable soup

②-③

about 200 g vegetables:
carrot, an onion, a small piece of celery or turnip, and a potato
25 g margarine
420 ml water or for extra flavour use stock
½ level teaspoon salt
shake pepper
1 level tablespoon flour
140 ml milk

1. Peel the vegetables thinly. Then, either put on to the chopping board and cut into neat small squares, generally called 'dice', or rub them against the coarse side of the grater, which is easier. Stand the grater on a large plate so that you do not make a mess on the table. (See picture, page 133.)
2. Heat the margarine in a saucepan and fry the vegetables in this.
3. Add the water or stock, salt and pepper.
4. Heat to simmering point, then cover saucepan and lower heat.
5. Simmer for 30 minutes with diced vegetables; grated vegetables are cooked in 20 minutes.
6. Put soup cups or a large soup dish to warm.
7. Put the flour into a basin and blend with the milk, add to the vegetable mixture and cook for 10 minutes, stirring all the time. Taste and add extra salt and pepper if necessary.
8. Spoon into the soup cups or dish.

Serve with bread or toast. Chopped parsley can be used as a garnish.

How to vary this soup

1. You can use only one kind of vegetable instead of a mixture. Carrots, onions, potatoes, all make good soup.

Vegetable soup (page 172)

2. Add a pinch of mixed herbs at stage 3.
3. Make the soup more creamy by using 280 ml water or stock at stage 3 and 280 ml milk at stage 7.

Canned soups

There are many kinds of canned soups. When you heat these, taste them carefully to see how you may add extra flavour. Sometimes a canned soup is nicer if you add a little milk or extra seasoning.

Dehydrated (dried) soups

Read the instructions on the packet about mixing and the quantity of water needed. *Cook for the times given* as the vegetables are *not* already cooked in these soups and need time to become soft and tender.

26. MAKING A STEAMED PUDDING

A STEAMED pudding is a good winter sweet, and you can give it many different flavours.

Before you make the pudding, turn back to page 139 and read again the important things about a 'rubbed in' mixture, for this is one way of mixing a pudding. You will see the mixture is very like that used for jam buns (pages 143–144). When the pudding is to be cooked, these are the things to remember:

1. Make sure that the water is boiling in the saucepan under the steamer, and look at this from time to time, as you will need to add more *boiling* water from the kettle.
2. See that the steamer is standing quite firmly on the saucepan so that it cannot be knocked off; this means choosing the right size saucepan.
3. The lid of the steamer should fit tightly so that the steam is kept inside.
4. You may not be using a steamer, in which case you will put a basin in a saucepan. You must be careful that the

water in the saucepan does not boil dry. Look often, and fill up with *boiling* water.

Jam pudding

2 tablespoons jam	②-③
100 g flour (self-raising or plain flour with 1 level teaspoon baking powder)	
50 g margarine	
50 g sugar	
1 egg	
about 2 tablespoons milk	

1. Grease a basin and put in the jam.
2. Sieve flour or flour and baking powder. Some people like to add a pinch of salt.
3. Rub in the margarine and add sugar. Break the egg into a small basin, beat with a fork and mix in with the other ingredients.
5. Stir in about 2 tablespoons milk. Look at the picture on page 174 and you will see how the mixture should look. It should just fall with the help of a spoon or knife.
6. Put into the basin over the jam.
7. Grease a round of greaseproof paper or foil, put it over the top of the pudding and tuck the edges in all round the pudding. You can see the beginning of this in the picture above.

8. Your teacher may want you to make a

Using oven gloves to turn out a steamed jam pudding

string handle so that you can easily lift the pudding out of the steamer, or you can put a folded band of foil under the basin in the steamer.

9. Put the pudding into the steamer, cover with the lid, carry over to the cooker and stand over the saucepan of boiling water.
10. Steam for $1\frac{1}{4}$ hours, filling up with boiling water.
11. Towards the end of the cooking time, put a serving plate or dish to warm.
12. Take the steamer off the saucepan, bring to the table, take out the basin and remove the paper or foil cover.
13. Put the serving plate on to the table. If the oven cloth or gloves are clean, use these as in this picture, or use a folded tea towel. Hold the basin firmly with the cloth in both hands, then turn over the plate. The pudding will fall out.

Serve with more hot jam or custard.

Other flavourings

1. Use golden syrup instead of jam.
2. Add 50–100 g chopped dates or other dried fruit to the mixture. The picture opposite shows a fruit pudding steamed in a fancy shape.

A steamed fruit pudding

3. Sieve $\frac{1}{2}$–1 level teaspoon mixed spice or powdered ginger with the flour.
4. Use 90 g flour and 15 g cocoa for a chocolate pudding.

Baked pudding

The same rubbed in mixture can be used for a baked pudding, which may be put over jam or fruit.

For jam, grease a pie-dish or ovenproof dish and put in the jam.

For fruit, prepare the fruit. (See page 103 on fruit puddings.) Put into the dish with sugar and a little water.

1. Make the pudding mixture. If it is to go over the fruit, which makes juice, use *barely* 2 tablespoons milk.
2. Spoon the pudding mixture over the fruit or the jam, as in the picture. Spread flat with a palette knife.
3. Bake in the centre of a moderate oven (180°C–Gas Mark 3–4) for hard fruits, and allow 45 minutes. For soft fruits and jam (190°C—Gas Mark 4–5) allow 35 minutes. The time will vary slightly according to the size of dish, so look into the oven before the end of the cooking time. The pudding should be firm and golden brown.

Serve with ice-cream, cream or custard.

What are its main food values?
steamed pudding

27. MEALS FOR ECONOMY

MEALS are planned to look and taste pleasant and to provide the important nutrients we must eat to keep healthy. They must also be planned to fit into the housekeeping budget. Many people think that only expensive food is *good* food. That is quite wrong; some of the most nutritious and delicious dishes are made from cheap foods.

Here are menus that would be inexpensive:

Hotpot, cabbage, baked custard, oven cooked fruit

Beef and vegetable stew, mashed potatoes, jam steamed pudding

Roast breast of lamb, roast potatoes, baked pudding over fruit

Fried or grilled herrings, bread and butter, mustard sauce, green salad, cheese and apples

Vegetable soup, fried or grilled cod, tomatoes, white sauce, potatoes, fresh fruit

It is economical to plan *how* you cook. For example:

If you are cooking a meal in the oven, you may have the right heat and space to cook fruit in a casserole or bake biscuits or cakes for another meal.

It is also wise housekeeping to make use of left-over food.

Left-over cheese, if it has become dry, should be grated and stored in covered jars in a cool place or a refrigerator. Use for cooking.

Left-over bread should be made into breadcrumbs. Rub the bread against the coarse side of the grater or through a sieve. Soft breadcrumbs will not keep but crisp breadcrumbs—often called raspings—do. Break bread, including crusts, into small pieces, put on to a baking tray or sheet and crisp in a very moderate oven (160°C—Gas Mark 3) until golden brown. Put on a piece of greaseproof paper, cover with another piece so the bread does not 'fly' about, then *roll slowly* with a rolling pin until you have fine crumbs. Store in covered jars: use for cooking.

28. BATTER

A BATTER is a mixture of flour, egg and milk. It has already been mentioned in this book, under Yorkshire pudding, which goes with beef (page 94). You can use a batter for many other different dishes: pancakes, about which you will be learning in a later book, and dishes such as toad-in-the-hole or Norfolk pudding, which are given here.

Batter

100 g flour, preferably plain	④
pinch salt	
1 egg	
280 ml milk	

(Sometimes people prefer to use part milk and part water; you must have 280 ml of liquid altogether.)

1. Sieve the flour and salt into a basin; choose one that is large enough for thorough beating when the liquid is being added. Beat with a wooden spoon.
2. Break the egg into a cup or small basin and pour into the flour.
3. Add about $\frac{1}{4}$ of the milk and stir carefully until the flour is blended with the egg and milk.
4. Beat really hard until you have a thick smooth mixture. It is now called a thick batter.
5. Some people like to let the thick batter stand before adding the rest of the liquid; others add the liquid straight away. Whichever method you use, pour the rest of the 280 ml liquid into the thick batter very slowly, beating all the time. When the liquid has nearly all been put in, you may like to change the wooden spoon for a flat whisk. The important thing is to beat well so that the batter does not become lumpy.
6. When all the liquid has been added, let the batter stand in a cool place until you are ready to use it.

Yorkshire pudding
Full instructions for baking Yorkshire pudding are given on page 94.

(Right) Norfolk pudding (page 18

Toad-in-the-hole

4–8 sausages ④
batter mixture (page 180), made with
100 g flour, etc.
15 g dripping or fat

(Use 8 sausages for a main meal, 4 sausages for supper.)

1. Grease the bottom of your Yorkshire pudding tin; the picture at the right shows an ideal tin to use for this.
2. Put in the sausages and bake for 10 minutes towards the top of a hot oven (220°C–Gas Mark 7).
3. Give the batter a final beat if it has been standing; pour it over the sausages.
4. Put back into the hot oven, but this time in the centre of the oven, to make sure the toad-in-the-hole cooks evenly at the top and bottom. Cook for a further 25–30 minutes, turning the heat down to moderate after 15 minutes to prevent burning.
5. Serve as quickly as possible after cooking. A batter can take the place of potatoes, so for a complete dinner serve

(Left) Grapefruit topped with a cherry (page 203)

with carrots and a green vegetable.
For supper, toad-in-the-hole could be served with tomatoes and a salad.

Norfolk pudding

This is very like a toad-in-the-hole except that you use fruit instead of sausages.

batter mixture (page 180), made with
100 g flour, etc.
$\frac{1}{2}$ kg apples
50 g sultanas
juice $\frac{1}{2}$ lemon
2 tablespoons sugar
25 g fat ④

1. Make the batter as recipe (page 180).
2. Grease the bottom and sides of an ovenproof dish, peel and slice the apples and arrange in the bottom. (See above.)
3. Add the sultanas, the juice of $\frac{1}{2}$ lemon and sugar. (See picture at right.)
4. Put towards the top of a hot oven for 10 minutes (220°C—Gas Mark 7).
5. Give the batter a final beat if it has been standing; pour it over the fruit.
6. Put back into the hot oven, but this time in the centre of the oven, to make sure that the pudding cooks evenly at the top and bottom. Cook for a further 25–30 minutes, turning the heat down to moderate after 15 minutes to prevent the pudding burning.
7. Serve immediately. Custard sauce goes well with this pudding. (See picture, page 181.)

What nutrients are found in these?

batter
toad-in-the-hole
Norfolk pudding

29. SCONES

SCONES are made by the 'rubbing in' method, but only a small amount of fat is used. This means that you need more milk and the dough is then kneaded lightly, rolled out and baked. You will remember in the rubbing in method, page 139, stage 4, it is mentioned that the liquid must be added *slowly*. This is very important for scones; if you have too much liquid, it will be difficult to roll out the dough.

The circled figure tells you the *number of scones* that can be made.

Plain scones

100 g flour (either self-raising, or plain flour with 1 level teaspoon baking powder) ④
pinch salt
15–25 g margarine   milk

(In scones, another kind of raising agent is often used instead of self-raising flour or plain flour with baking powder.

To 100 g plain flour you can use:
$\frac{1}{4}$ level teaspoon of bicarbonate of soda
$\frac{1}{2}$ level teaspoon of cream of tartar

It is important that you get these quantities quite correct, as too much will give an unpleasant taste to the scones; too little will stop them rising properly, so take care in measuring.)

1. Sieve *either*
   the self-raising flour and salt, *or*
   flour, salt and baking powder, *or*
   flour, bicarbonate of soda, cream of tartar and salt
   into a bowl.
2. Rub the fat into the flour as described in the rubbed in method (page 139).
3. Add 2 tablespoons of milk, mix with the flour and fat, using a palette knife. Add another tablespoon of milk and mix again. You will find that the dough is beginning to come together. For this quantity of flour you will need approximately 4 tablespoons of milk, but add the fourth tablespoon very slowly so that you do not put in too much.

8. When you have a neat round, mark this into 4 sections. (See the picture below.)
9. This is ready to go on to the baking sheet or baking tray. A plain scone like this could be baked on an ungreased baking tray, but some people prefer greasing the tray. Put the scone on the tray; it is then ready to be baked.
10. A whole scone round, as this is called, should be baked just above the middle of the oven. If your teacher tells you to separate the 4 sections into triangles, as the cheese scones in the picture opposite,

4. The dough is ready when it will form a ball and leave your mixing bowl clean.
5. Put down the palette knife and use the tips of your fingers to gather the dough together.
6. Shake a little flour from the flour sifter or flour dredger on to your pastry board, put the ball of scone dough on to the board and shake a small amount of flour over the rolling pin.
7. Roll the scone dough out gently and firmly into a round, as shown above. If the edges of the round get untidy, just neaten them with your hands.

you could bake these towards the top of the oven as they cook more quickly.
11. Bake a scone round for approximately 15–20 minutes in a hot oven (220°C—Gas Mark 7). Bake individual scones for 10–12 minutes towards the top of a hot oven.
12. Lift from the baking sheet or tray on to a wire cooling tray.
13. Serve scones hot or cold, with butter and jam.

How to vary scones

1. *A sweet scone*
Add 1 tablespoon of sugar to the flour and fat mixture *after* rubbing in.
Instead of sugar, use 1 tablespoon honey, golden syrup or black treacle. You will then need less milk.

2. *Fruit scones*
Add 1 tablespoon sugar and 1 tablespoon currants, sultanas, or mixed fruit—to the rubbed in mixture.

3. *Cheese scones*
Sieve $\frac{1}{4}$ level teaspoon salt, a shake of pepper and a pinch of dry mustard with the flour.
Rub in the fat, add 25 g finely grated cheese, then mix with the milk.

What are their main food values?

a plain scone
a fruit scone
a cheese scone

What would you serve with scones for tea to make a more nourishing meal?

30. PASTRY

DO not be impatient when you first make pastry if you find it more difficult than the other rubbed in mixtures. It is not so easy because it is very important that you have the mixture the right consistency; this means it is neither too wet nor too dry. It is also important to handle pastry carefully. If you use the rolling pin too heavily, you make pastry rather heavy, so practise rolling it out gently as well as firmly.

Shortcrust pastry

100 g flour, preferably plain
pinch salt, 50 g fat
cold water, approximately 1 tablespoon

(People vary in the fat they like to use in shortcrust pastry; your teacher will tell you what she would like you to use. It may be: 25 g margarine and 25 g lard *or* 25 g margarine and 25 g cooking fat; *or* it may be all margarine; *or* all fat, lard or cooking fat; *or* all butter.)

1. Sieve the flour and salt into a mixing bowl.
2. Rub the fat or margarine and fat in with the tips of your fingers, as described in the rubbing in mixture (page 139).
3. Look back to the picture of rubbing in on page 138.
4. Add the water very gradually; 1 tablespoon is approximately the amount you will need to make the mixture bind together (bind means hold together and form into a ball).

5. The picture on page 189 shows how you mix this water in with the flour and fat.
6. The pastry is the right consistency when you can push it into this ball without any difficulty.
7. Shake the flour dredger or flour sifter over the pastry board lightly; put the ball of pastry dough on to this.
8. Shake a very little flour over the rolling pin and roll the pastry out lightly and firmly; the picture above shows the way to hold the rolling pin so that you press down firmly but not too heavily.
9. The pastry is then ready to use.

Jam turnover

One of the nicest and easiest ways of using shortcrust pastry is in a jam turnover. For 1 jam turnover you need:

shortcrust pastry made with
100 g flour (see page 189)
1 good tablespoon jam

1. Roll the pastry until it is a neat square.
2. Cut away any untidy edges; you may have to waste these for a turnover, but when you make pies and tarts these could be used. Try to waste as little as possible. (See picture opposite.)
3. Put the spoonful of jam in the centre of the square (picture 2).
4. Brush the edges of the pastry with a little water.
5. Fold over into a triangle (picture 3).
6. Press the edges together with a fork (picture 4). This prevents the jam from running out when the turnover is cooked.
7. Lift the turnover on to a lightly greased baking sheet or tray. The easiest way to do this is to slip a palette knife or fish slice under the pastry.

3
4

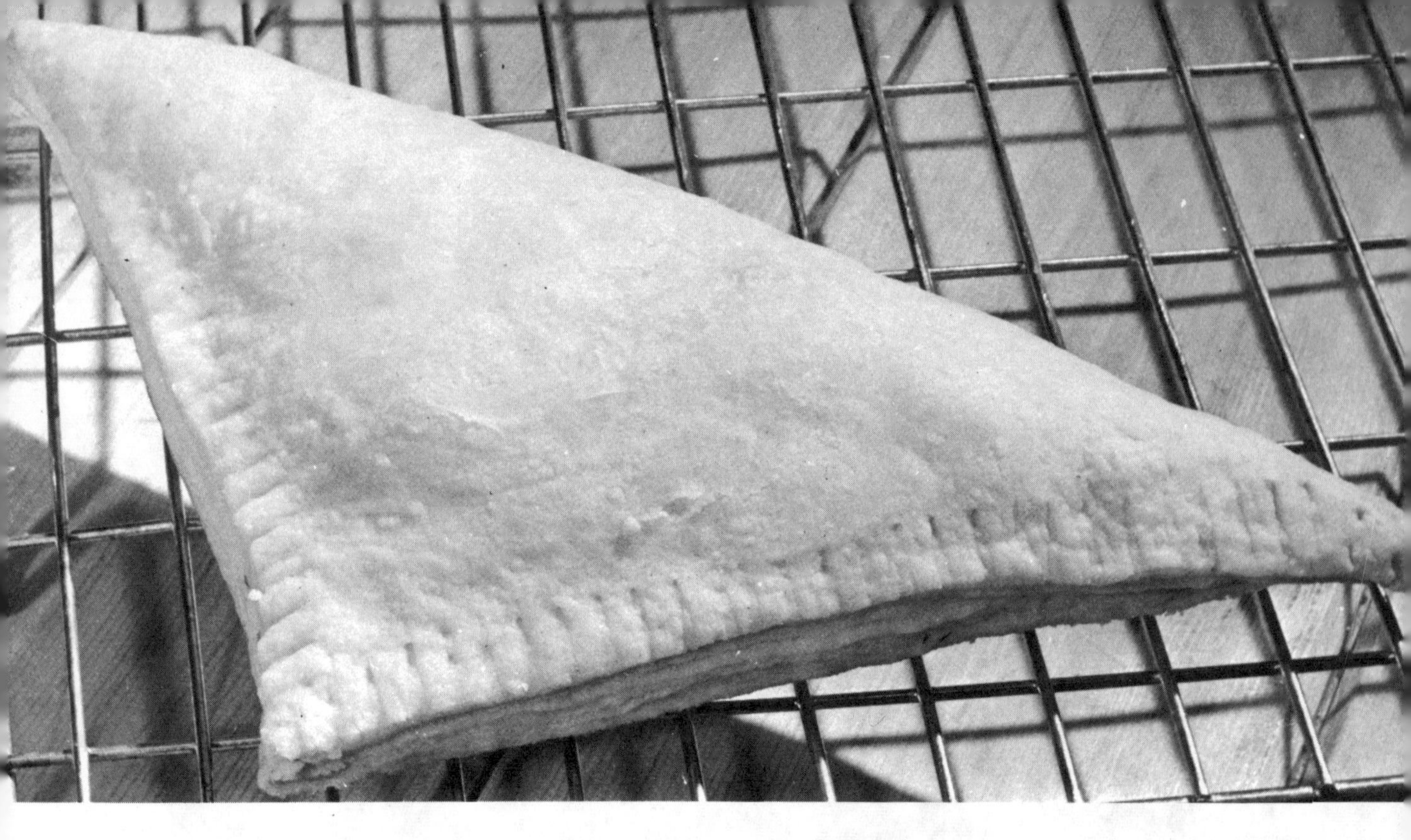

8. Bake in the centre of a moderately hot oven (200°C—Gas Mark 6) for approximately 20 minutes until the pastry is golden brown and crisp.

9. Take the tray out of the oven, lift the pastry off and put it on to a wire cooling tray (picture above).

10. Serve hot or cold.

31. MAKING FOODS MORE INTERESTING

MOST of the simple dishes have been described in this book, but there are ways in which the simplest dish can be made more interesting.

Stuffing adds flavour

For example, the picture on the right shows steaks or cutlets of cod, and on page 121 are instructions for baking cod. These dishes would be much more interesting if the fish were baked with stuffing. You can use a sage and onion stuffing (page 95), or make up packet stuffing. All you need do is to put the stuffing on to the pieces of fish, after cutting away the bone, as shown in the picture.

Stuffed fillets of herring

Herrings are much more interesting if they are stuffed.

Method 1

Make up packet stuffing or use sage and onion stuffing (page 95). Split the herring, remove the bone; the picture on page 124

shows how you do this. Spread the stuffing over the herring and then put it in the dish to bake.
Where stuffings are added to foods, the dish takes a little longer to cook.

Method 2
Another way to stuff herring is shown in these two pictures. Split and bone the herring as on page 124, then cut the fish into two fillets.
The picture above shows the stuffing being put on one fillet; it is then rolled and baked. Fillets of herring stuffed (picture below) will need only a good 15 minutes, whereas whole stuffed herring wants 20 minutes.

Stuffed jacket potatoes

1 potato ①
1 rasher bacon
1 tomato

These are more interesting and become a more complete meal if stuffed. Page 72 tells you how to stuff a potato with cheese. You could use chopped fried bacon and fried tomatoes.

1. Cook the potato as the recipe (page 71).
2. Remove the rind from the bacon and cut the bacon into tiny pieces; fry for a few minutes and add the skinned, sliced tomato.
3. Take the cooked potato out of the oven and cut a slice off the top of this; scoop out the pulp, put it into a basin and mash.
4. Mix with the bacon, tomato, a pinch of salt and a shake of pepper.
5. Pile back into the potato case, and heat for 10 minutes in the oven.

Decoration makes food more interesting

On page 136 are instructions for making a fruit crumble, and the picture on this page shows how that crumble can be made into a very interesting-looking dish. When the pudding is baked, decorate it with half glacé cherries and small pieces

of angelica cut into a diamond shape to look like leaves. You can serve it, as in the picture on page 195, with a creamy topping mix (Dream topping).

Colour makes food more interesting

The picture at the left shows how sandwiches look more exciting if the filling is placed on one slice of bread and butter rather than between two slices. Types of food that can be put on open sandwiches to give colour are:

- egg, hard-boiled and cut into slices
- sardines
- ham or luncheon meat

Remember, pieces of parsley and small lettuce leaves also help to make food more interesting.

Mixing flavours

Choose chocolate ice-cream and decorate it with whipped cream or Dream topping, as in the picture. Add slices of banana (dipped in a little lemon juice to keep them white), a glacé cherry and half a wafer biscuit.

It is *fun* working out new ideas in mixing flavours; try for yourself.

An ice-cream sweet for a special occasion

32. MEALS IN A HURRY

THE fact that you make a meal in a hurry does not mean it need contain little food value. If you plan carefully, referring to Chapter One, you can prepare very nutritious meals in a short time.

In addition, a quickly made meal should look attractive and have a good flavour. Here are some ideas; you will be able to think of others.

1. *Egg dishes* are quick to prepare. Serve with a salad, with beans or spaghetti.

2. Most *fish dishes* cook quickly, particularly if fried.

3. *Chops, steaks, sausages and bacon* are meats that need shorter cooking time. To make a complete meal, serve with canned beans or spaghetti, and crisps.

4. *Frozen prepared meats* such as hamburgers or meat cakes are also useful if you have little cooking time.

5. *Simple salads* with cheese or canned fish are a good choice when you are short of time. To make the meal more substantial, serve canned or powdered soup and finish the meal with fresh fruit.

6. *Cheese,* uncooked, either with salad or with rolls or bread and butter, is one of the quickest of meals, and it is a nourishing meal if followed with fresh fruit.

A snack meal for a special occasion is shown opposite: canned spaghetti in tomato and cheese sauce on sausage meat-cakes and toast; grapefruit and ginger (page 203).

33. MEALS FOR A PARTY

If you are preparing food for a party, do not imagine that you must prepare very difficult dishes. Many of the recipes you have learned in this book can be made quite suitable.

Savoury dishes for a party

Sandwiches

The picture opposite shows how attractive simple sandwiches can be.

On the *light plate*, you have an interesting and unusual mixture of jam and cream cheese spread. Cover one slice of bread with cream cheese spread instead of butter; butter the other slice of bread, cover with jam, put the two together and cut into neat triangles.

On the *dark plate*, the bread is spread with cream cheese and the sandwiches filled with tomato and cucumber. By allowing the different colour to show, the sandwiches are much more interesting.

The *rolled sandwiches* are not difficult to make. Cut slices of bread and spread with cream cheese. Remove the crusts, put a piece of ham on top of the cream cheese and roll firmly. Cut into slices and put wooden cocktail sticks through them.

Make the sandwiches look gay with slices of tomato, parsley or lettuce to garnish. For a large party, buy small sandwich flags and write on them neatly the name of the filling.

Salads

Salads with cold ham or hard-boiled egg and sardines are suitable for a summer party. Take special trouble to make these look pretty.

If you have to plan a complete meal for a party, choose very attractive colourful vegetables.

Sweets for a party

Fruit salad is one of the nicest sweets for a party. One way of making it is given on page 105, but the picture overleaf shows how attractive this fruit salad can be with a mixture of canned, dried and fresh fruits.

A very simple fruit salad can be made with three or four fruits only, e.g. oranges cut in segments or rings, bananas cut in neat slices, canned or glacé cherries to give colour, and apples or pears cut into slices. When you prepare an orange for a fruit salad, the best way is to cut the peel away from the fruit rather thickly as shown below. This means you take away all the white pith.

For segments: cut *between* the pieces of skin.
For slices: cut *across* the orange. Squeeze the peel very hard to take out any juice remaining.

Another sweet for a party could be fruit snow or fruit fool. (See recipes, pages 105 and 107, picture, page 109.)

Party Snack

Sometimes you may have to serve a snack meal for guests. The picture on page 199 gives you some good ideas for this.

If you have friends staying and you want an interesting breakfast, first serve:

Grapefruit

It can be topped with a cherry (picture, page 182), or with chopped ginger (page 199).

Sausage cakes or hamburgers on rounds of toast, topped with spaghetti

To make sausage cakes, buy sausagemeat instead of sausages, form into even neat rounds, fry or grill these just as you would sausages. Put on top of the pieces of toast and cover with spaghetti in tomato and cheese sauce (page 199).

At breakfast time you also serve crisp toast and marmalade.

This meal would be just as good for dinner, but instead of the toast and marmalade, you could have grilled or fried tomatoes and a green salad.

You could serve it for supper, with tomatoes and potato crisps.

If you are having a party, you must plan what you are giving people to drink as well as to eat.
Choose your nicest china; make sure the coffee or tea is made really well and that it is hot and served as well as possible. (See picture, page 203.)
In addition to coffee and/or tea, you may like to include fruit drinks. Recipes for these are on pages 108, 111.
The important thing about giving a party is to plan well ahead; make all the preparations as early as you can, so that when your guests arrive there is no fuss or bother, and everyone can enjoy the occasion.

SHOPPING

ON the following pages you will find nearly all the foods that have been mentioned in this book. They are in the form of a shopping list. When you go shopping for yourself, for your mother or teacher, there are certain things to remember. If you always do these, you will find that shopping is more enjoyable, you waste less time, and certainly become a better manager.

1. Get in the habit of looking round the store-cupboard, refrigerator and kitchen, and make a note of supplies that are running low. When you open the last packet of sugar, it is time to buy more. Keep a book or a pad handy and put down things needed.
2. Make a shopping list before you leave. This prevents you forgetting anything.
3. If you live a long way from the shops, you will naturally have to buy supplies for several days, but never buy more food than you can use while it is in good condition. It is a waste of money to keep food so long that it spoils.
4. Get to know the various shopkeepers. You will find that the butcher will help you to recognise the cuts of meat; the greengrocer will tell you about the more unusual fruits if you ask him when he is not too busy.
5. When you are buying foods that are sold by weight, watch the scales to make sure the assistant does not make a mistake.
6. Check your change as the assistant gives it to you; if a mistake has been made, it can be put right at once.
7. In arithmetic you will be given examples of how to work out the cost per dozen, so practise doing this to help your shopping. For example, if potatoes are 8p per kg then 6 kg would cost 48p (6 times 8p); or if eggs cost 24p per dozen, then each egg costs 2p.

STORING FOODS

In the shopping list you are given brief instructions on how to store. Many people today have refrigerators as well as larders or pantries, and it is important to realise that a refrigerator will only keep food in good condition if you follow these rules:

1. Cover all foods in a refrigerator except raw meat.
2. Keep strongly smelling foods such as fish immediately under the ice-making compartment. This prevents the smell of the fish being taken round the refrigerator and spoiling other foods.

3. Take particular care to cover dairy produce —milk, cream, butter—so that it does not spoil in taste.
4. Salads should be put either in the salad container or wrapped in foil or plastic bags, as a certain amount of moisture is needed to keep them crisp. *Never* put lettuce, tomatoes and other salads just on the shelves of the refrigerator.
5. Never put very hot foods or liquids into the refrigerator; wait until they have cooled.
6. Always store frozen foods and ice-cream in the ice-making compartment. They do not keep in the ordinary part of the refrigerator.
7. A refrigerator will only work properly if it is kept defrosted regularly. This means getting rid of the layer of ice round the ice-making compartment when it is about 1 cm thick. Your teacher will tell you how to do this, or you can read about it in the book belonging to your refrigerator.
8. When you defrost the refrigerator, take food out and wipe the inside with warm water. You can add a few drops of vinegar or a teaspoon of bicarbonate of soda to the water. Do not use soap or soapless detergents, as these might leave a smell.

The larder should be kept clean and well ventilated, and the foods covered as instructed.

MEATS

Buying fresh meat

The meat should look firm and bright in colour and should smell fresh. The shop should look clean.

To store

Uncooked meat should be kept *uncovered* in refrigerator; when cooked, it must be covered to prevent it drying. When storing in a ventilated larder, cover with a meat safe or muslin. In hot weather, wash meat in vinegar water: 1 tablespoon vinegar to 560 ml water.

These are the meats sold uncooked:

beef, mutton, lamb, pork, veal

Decide how you wish to cook the meat, then look up pages 87-97 for roasting, pages 98-102 for frying and grilling, and pages 165-169 for stewing. If in doubt as to a suitable cut, ask the butcher.

Sausages

Pork sausages are dearer than beef; you get approximately 8 large sausages to $\frac{1}{2}$ kg.

Liver

This is one of the meats called *offal*. If you buy

for frying, ask for calf's, lamb's or pig's liver. Ox liver is suitable only for stewing.

Bacon
For frying or grilling, for breakfast or tea, choose either streaky rashers, which are the cheapest but sometimes rather fat so look at them carefully, *or* back rashers. Gammon rashers are more expensive and would be suitable for a main meal.

Cooked ham
Sometimes ham is already sliced and left on the shop counter, where it becomes dry. If the lean part is brown and not pink, the ham is stale. Do not buy it like this but ask for fresh.

FISH

Buying fresh fish
This should be firm, smell pleasant; a strong smell of ammonia means the fish is stale. Scales on herrings should be bright silver.

To store
In a refrigerator, store as near the ice-making compartment as possible and cover. (See page 206.) Do not store in a larder for long; cover with muslin or a meat safe.

WHITE FISH

Cod, fresh haddock, hake
Cutlets, sometimes called steaks, or pieces of fillet; cod is the cheapest.

Rock salmon
Cheap fish; buy pieces of fillet.

Plaice, sole (flat fish)
Buy whole or fillets, fairly expensive.

Whiting
Buy whole or filleted.

SMOKED FISH

Haddock
Buy small whole fish, or larger ones filleted.

Cod
Buy pieces of fillet.

Kippers
These are often sold in pairs or buy filleted.

OILY FISH

Herrings, mackerel
Buy whole fish. Fishmongers will split and bone.

Bloaters
These are a kind of smoked herring.

Sprats
These are like very small herrings.

CANNED FISH

Sardines, tuna, salmon
Use in salads or sandwiches (pages 48, 85).

SHELLFISH

Lobster, crab, prawns, shrimps, etc.
These are generally sold ready cooked.

DAIRY PRODUCE

Store in a cool, dry place. Cover in the refrigerator to prevent them drying, or put in the special compartment.

BUTTER

In packets, salted or unsalted; *Australian* and *New Zealand* are among the cheapest kinds.

CHEESE

The most popular varieties are:
Cheddar, for eating and cooking. This should be firm not hard and dry; mild or strong; sold by weight, sometimes ready packed.
Cheshire, generally white; for eating and cooking.
Processed, portions or slices; good for sandwiches; some can be used in cooking.
Cream cheese and *cream cheese spread,* excellent for sandwiches; store in a cool place.
There are many other kinds of cheese made in Britain, or coming from abroad. Buy small amounts of these, as well as the cheeses mentioned here.

MILK

Fresh milk is bought in sealed containers; Channel Island milk is the most expensive.

Canned milk
(a) *Evaporated* is unsweetened; use in place of cream or dilute with water to use in place of fresh milk.

(b) *Condensed milk* is sweetened; use in tea or coffee, or dilute with water as sweetened milk.

Sterilised milk looks like fresh milk, is sold in sealed bottles and keeps for some days. Long-life milk, sold in cartons, keeps some months.

Powdered milk is sold in tins; add the powder direct to tea or coffee, or mix with water to use in place of fresh milk.

Cream Some shops sell thin cream as well as thick (double) cream and sometimes whipping cream too.

EGGS

There are 4 sizes: *large, medium, standard, small.* Buy small eggs for young children; use standard or small eggs in plain cakes.

VEGETABLES

Store in a well-ventilated place.

ROOT VEGETABLES

Carrots, turnips, swedes, parsnips, potatoes
They should be firm and unblemished. Avoid those with cracks; sold by weight. They keep well, but less well when washed and packed in plastic bags.

Celery
Look for large firm inner sticks (heart).

Onions
Buy some small to use just for flavouring.

Beetroot
(a) Cooked, firm not damp or sticky; (b) Uncooked, without marks.

GREEN VEGETABLES

Cabbage, cabbage greens, sprouts, lettuce
They should be green and firm, and feel heavy for their size. Do not buy if the leaves are yellow.

Cauliflower
This should have a firm white flower (curd).

Spinach
This should be firm and green. As it reduces in cooking, you will need about 1 kg for 4 portions.

Peas, beans
They should be firm and green. If *runner beans* and *French beans* are hard and large they will be tough. Broad beans are best when not big.

SALAD VEGETABLES, HERBS, etc.

Tomatoes
Firm with no splits.

Cucumber
Firm, green, not yellow skin.

Watercress, parsley, mint
Leaves should be bright green and crisp.

Mushrooms
Firm, not flabby. The tiny ones are ' button ' mushrooms; the larger ones ' flats '.

DRIED VEGETABLES

Butter or haricot beans, lentils
Bought in packets or loose. Keep in cool dry place. Quick cooking *dried vegetables* can also be bought. (See page 68.)

FRUITS

Store in a cool well-ventilated place.

Apples
They should be firm and unblemished.

Bananas
They are easier to digest if brown flecked or nearly black. If greenish, they are under-ripe.

Grapes
Check that all in the bunch are perfect.

Pears
Do not buy too ripe. They should feel soft when pressed gently at the stalk end.

Rhubarb
This should have firm, not limp, stalks.

SOFT FRUITS

Strawberries, gooseberries, black and red currants, raspberries and loganberries
These fruits should be firm. If soft and wet, they are stale or have been picked on a wet day and will not keep.

CITRUS FRUITS

Oranges, lemons, grapefruit
If they feel heavy for their size, they are full of juice.

DRIED FRUITS

Figs, dates
These are sold in boxes for eating and in packets for chopping and cooking.

FATS

Cooking fat or *lard*
Used in frying, etc. (See page 160.) Buy in packets.

Margarine
Buy in packets. The more expensive kinds have a little butter added.

Suet
Use in dumplings, etc. Buy in packets ready shredded or from the butcher. This has to be chopped.

BREAD

Put in a bread bin or metal-lined drawer, or wrap in foil or a clean tea cloth. Ready-wrapped bread keeps moister.

White bread
Sliced and wrapped (a) *thin* for bread and butter, and (b) *thick* for toast. Unsliced, for cutting at home.

Brown bread
As white

Wholemeal
This is rarely sold ready sliced.

CANNED FOODS

Put in a cool dry place. If they bulge at the end, which rarely happens, do not buy. When the can is opened, store in a cool place and use quickly.

Fish
See page 115.

Milk
See page 75.

Here are some of the other canned foods mentioned in this book.

Fruits and fruit juices
Various flavours and sizes. Remove from can if any is left as the syrup goes cloudy.

Milk puddings
In various sizes, ready to eat.

Spaghetti, baked beans
Sold from individual sizes upwards, in tomato and cheese sauce. Heat as directed on the can.

Vegetables—peas, beans, carrots, etc.
Various sizes (already cooked). Heat as directed on the can.

FROZEN FOODS

1. You can buy frozen fish, meats, vegetables, fruits, pastry and cakes. The most popular frozen food is, of course, *ice-cream*.
2. When you buy frozen foods, look at the cabinet in the shop. There is a line inside. If the foods are below this line, they are stored in the right temperature; if above, the temperature is too high. Do *not* buy them.
3. If food becomes very soft and completely defrosted, do not try to re-freeze in the refrigerator.
4. Packets must be stored in the ice-making compartment of the refrigerator.

DETERGENTS

This is the word that covers many cleaning products. You can buy powdered detergents or liquid detergents. Soap is also a detergent.

GREASEPROOF PAPER, FOIL

These goods are sold in packets or rolls. *Kitchen paper* is sold in the same way.

GROCERIES

These are listed on page 212 in alphabetical order.
Store them carefully in a cool dry place. Label bins of flour, etc.

GROCERIES

Angelica, becomes sticky if left too long. Don't buy too much.
Baking powder, in tins or packets
Bicarbonate of soda, in packets
Black treacle, in tins. Keep the lid on.
Black currant syrup, in bottles
Blancmange, in tins or packets
Cereal, in packets
Coffee, whole beans which need grinding, ready ground coffee, or instant coffee in tins
Cocoa and *chocolate,* in tins or packets
Cornflour, in tins or packets
Cream of tartar, in packets
Custard powder, in tins or packets
DRIED FRUITS, *sultanas, currants, raisins, prunes, apricots,* loose by weight or in packets
Flour, plain and *self-raising,* in $\frac{1}{2}$ kg and $1\frac{1}{2}$ kg bags. Perhaps larger quantities in school.
Gelatine, in packets containing about 15 g envelopes.
Glace cherries, see angelica
Golden syrup, in tins. Keep the lid on.
Gravy browning, in tins or packets
Honey, as jam
Horseradish sauce, in jars
Jam; marmalade, in jars. Replace the lid.
Jelly, in packets to make 560 ml
Macaroni, in packets
Mayonnaise, in bottles
Mixed spice, in small drums (round containers)
Mustard, dry in tins. Blend with water or milk. Ready-mixed in jars or tubes.
Nutmeg, whole for grating, or ready grated
Oatmeal, rolled oats, for porridge. Sold in packets.
Oil, in bottles. Olive oil or corn oil are the most usual kinds.
Packet stuffing, keep dry.
Pepper, in drums, ready ground, or peppercorns for grinding.
Puddings, see page 77, 83.
Rice, loose or in packets. Round for puddings and long for savouries.
Rose hip syrup, in bottles
Salt, table salt in drums. Kitchen salt (cheaper) in blocks. Crush and put in jars.
Sugar, white—granulated, coarse grain. *Castor* (more expensive), fine grain for light cakes. *Icing,* for cakes. *Loaf,* for tea and coffee. *Brown,* various kinds. The most usual is *demerara.*
Stock cubes, small cubes
Tea, in packets
Toppings, see page 82.
Vanilla essence, in small bottles
Vinegar, in bottles. White or brown malt

INDEX

Figures in italics refer to coloured pictures